Effect of relaxation … n on patients with coronary heart disease

Mary Iby. P

CONTENTS

CERTIFICATE
DECLARATION
ACKNOWLEDGEMENTS
LIST OF TABLES
LIST OF FIGURES

CHAPTER		PAGE
I	INTRODUCTION	1
II	REVIEW OF LITERATURE	17
III	METHODOLOGY	79
IV	RESULTS AND DISCUSSION	118
V	SUMMARY AND CONCLUSIONS	159
	REFERENCES	172
	APPENDICES	198

CHAPTER I

INTRODUCTION

A. Importance of the investigation
B. Statement of the problem
C. Hypotheses
D. Methodology in brief
E. Organization of the report

A. IMPORTANCE OF THE INVESTIGATION

Coronary Heart Disease (CHD) or Coronary Artery Disease or Ischaemic Heart Disease is now proving to be one of the leading causes of morbidity and mortality throughout the world. The main cause of this disease is deposition of cholesterol and fat in the inner smooth lining of the blood vessels (coronary arteries) supplying blood to the heart resulting in their blockages and obstruction to blood flow through them. With significant blockages, more than 60 to 70 per cent, and exertion, the increased demand of blood by the heart is not met, and a sensation of pain is felt in the chest, usually called angina. Angina, more specifically, is the sensation of heaviness or pain in the left side of the chest which typically radiates to the left arm and may be associated with sweating, choking sensation, and breathlessness. Less often, the pain may occur on the right side of the chest, shoulders, and even the lower jaws or teeth.

This is a very dreaded condition, and if left unattended to may give rise to life threatening consequences. More than one-sixth of all people killed by heart disease are under the age of 65.Annually, between 250,000 and 300,000 heart attack victims die before reaching a hospital.

The incidence of cardiovascular disease in India according to an estimated figure of 1991 has been 4.04 crore, and this figure touched 5.25 crore by 2001. It has been predicted that cardiovascular disease will be the most important cause of mortality in India by the year 2015. It is more prevalent among the younger population as a larger number of people in their 30's and 40's are affected. Two new cases of CHD are being detected each hour in Delhi. If Delhi were to represent what is happening in urban India, then 100 new cases of heart disease increase every hour, meaning roughly 2500 cases each day.

Forty million people in USA suffer from diagnosed cardiovascular disease, and an even larger number don't yet know that they have a heart problem. Sixty million people have high blood pressure. Eighty million have elevated cholesterol levels. Over 1.5 million Americans have heart attacks every year. And for almost one third of them, having a heart attack was their first indication that they had a heart problem.

The World Health Organization reports that the number of deaths from heart attacks and strokes in India are projected to increase to 70 lakhs by 2020 (Express Features, 2003). Although lifestyle factors play a major role, medication to lower blood pressure and prevent cholesterol or reverse heart disease is being considered by only a small percentage of people. Comprehensive lifestyle programme can lower cholesterol and blood pressure, more than has ever been reported without drugs and can even begin to reverse severe coronary heart disease in many people without using cholesterol-lowering drugs or surgery.

Certain conditions and lifestyle habits are now recognized to be responsible for the deposition of cholesterol and fat in blood vessels as well as the increased rate at which they are being deposited. These are generally referred to as risk factors, and can be divided into two categories: 1. Modifiable risk factors: In this group come those risk factors which can be altered and prevented so that further progress of heart disease can be arrested, e.g. stress, blood pressure, cholesterol etc. 2. Non-modifiable risk factors include risk factors which cannot be altered, such as age, sex, and heredity (Kapadia, 1996).

Studies have shown that negative emotions such as anger, hatred, resentment, jealousy, pride, egoism, anxiety, depression, and insecurity decrease the heart rate variability (HRV is the fluctuation of the heart rate around a mean heart rate - the time between beats. This beat to beat time variation is called HRV. Positive emotions allow a smooth, even, and harmonious HRV. Negative emotions cause erratic and non-harmonious HRV, and increase 5-fold the proneness to sudden death, in the patients with history of heart attack.

There are a number of changes which cause stress, e.g., failure in studies, death of a parent or a dear one, prolonged illness of a member of the family, a serious accident, financial crisis, etc. All these have their effect upon the coronary circulation. This happens due to biochemical changes in the body, increased secretion of catecholamine and increase in sympathetic tone.

The coronary arteries respond to the stressful changes with contraction of their muscles resulting in the narrowing of their lumen. The blood circulating in the coronary arteries also becomes thicker in consistency in response to stress. They also increase viscosity of blood due to increase in stickiness of the platelets. These occur through various chemical and neuro-hormonal reactions. These emotions also affect the health of the immune system and make the body prone to ill-health in general. It is now realized that the effect of any stress depends upon its perception by the individual. In other words, what a person makes of that situation is important. The positive emotions of caring, love, compassion, and altruism promote healthy biochemical reactions leading to good health and longevity.

Studies indicated that emotional stress increases blood pressure and blood levels of cholesterol independent of diet-the type of stress is not that important. Indianapolis 500 racecar drivers have higher cholesterol levels after the race than before. Medical students have higher cholesterol levels during examinations (Ornish, 1996).

A patient of coronary heart disease may have a strong family history, may be overweight, may be sedentary in habits, may be a heavy smoker or may be drinking alcohol in excess. He may have high serum cholesterol and may be suffering from diabetes and hypertension. If not all these, he may be overstressed with a lack of social support and feel isolated.

Psychological stress or tension is now recognized as the most important risk factor of coronary heart disease. With more and more scientific research results pouring in over the last two to three decades, the excessive stress can lead to the following: Increase in Blood Pressure, Increase in the Heart Rate, Increased concentration of fat in blood, Increased blood sugar, Increased cholesterol in blood, Spasm of coronary and other arteries, Increased blood clotting and Increased deposition of fat and cholesterol in the arteries. This means that stress is such an influential risk factor that even in the absence of other risk factors it can itself become responsible for coronary heart disease.

There are many people without high cholesterol, overweight and family history, having normal blood pressure developing angina only because of excessive stress.

Ornish's programme emphasizes stress management sessions. Each session is led by an instructor trained in Ornish's techniques of stress management, including stretching exercises, breathing techniques, meditation, creative visualization and progressive relaxation.

Effectively managing emotional stress helps eliminate one of the risk factors involved in heart disease, and facilitates physical, mental, and spiritual wellness. Many participants report the rewards of making big changes such as these are well worth the time invested. Often, chest pain diminishes markedly, serum cholesterol drops, blood pressure stabilizes at a reduced level, medications are reduced or eliminated, participants begin to lose weight and report a renewed sense of confidence and control and many of these changes usually become apparent within a short period of time.

Psychological factors such as depression, anxiety, and hostility may influence the development, clinical expression, and prognosis of heart disease. Accordingly, it is critical that clinically significant levels of distress are identified, both in hospital and after discharge, to target patients who require specific psychological intervention, in addition to conventional cardiac rehabilitation.

Studies have shown that up to one fifth of patients with coronary heart disease may have concomitant major depression (Smith, 1993; Carney, 1987; 1990; Scheifler et al., 1989). Depression may also be considered a risk factor for developing cardiac disease (Avery & Winokur, 1976; Pratt et al., 1996; Anda et al., 1993). It is useful therefore to explore more fully the data that link psychological variables to cardiovascular disease and speculate on the underlying pathophysiologic mechanisms.

It may be remembered that one way to examine the adequacy of the evidence relating variables such as depression and anxiety to cardiovascular disease is to use classic epidemiologic principles to assess causality. The main criteria used to assessment are strength of association (risk ratio), dose-response relationships, consistency of association, and temporally correct association.

Some current studies relating depression to coronary heart disease have methodological weaknesses that make assessing the strength of the association inconclusive. When psychiatric diagnostic instruments that have not been modified are used to determine the prevalence of depression, they may not have the same validity for patients with CHD as they do in the general population. Excluding some patients because of the severity of their cardiovascular disease and measuring depressive symptoms at different times after hospital admission also reduce the validity of the analysis.

However, certain studies are relatively well controlled, are prospective in design, use structural clinical interviews with diagnostic instruments, include other risk factors for CHD in their analysis, and control for demographic factors. (Pratt et al., 1996; Anda et al., 1993; Smoller et al., 1996; Aromaa et al., 1994; Barefoot et al., 1996; Carney et al., 1988; Denollet et al., 1996; Everson et al., 1996; Kennedy et al., 1987). Patients with more severe anxiety have been shown to develop more severe CHD.

Kawachi et al. (1994) published data on a prospective study of phobic anxiety and the risk of CHD in men. Thirty-four thousand male health professionals who were initially free of cardiovascular disease at baseline were assessed using he Crown-Crisp Experiential Index. The age-adjusted relative risk of fatal CHD was significantly different when the highest and lowest subsets were compared and adjusted for other potentially confounding variables. Interestingly, the excess risk was confined to sudden death. The study did not, however, measure other personality or psychiatric variables such as indices of depression.

A more recent literature review cites 10 prospective studies linking anxiety to coronary heart disease. Thus, the evidence for a link between anxiety and CHD is a compelling as that available for a link between depression and CHD.

While describing "a conceptual model of the pathophysiologic actions of acute and chronic stress in CHD", it has been stated that mental stress, either acute or chronic, produces certain physiologic responses via the central nervous system. These physiologic responses consist of increases in catecholamine, heart rate, and blood pressure, increased coronary constriction; and increased platelet activity. The cardiac effects of these responses are modified by background factors including atherosclerosis, prior myocardial infarction, and poor left ventricular function. These cardiac effects can raise electrical instability, thereby triggering arrhythmias. This, in turn, may lead to sudden cardiac death, increased myocardial oxygen demand that can result in ischemia, or decreased myocardial oxygen supply that can also result in ischemia, leading to either sudden cardiac death or myocardial infarction.

In addition, acute changes in haemodynamics and neurohormonal levels can occur. An acute rise in blood pressure and catecholamines precipitates plaque rupture and coronary thrombosis resulting in myocardial infarction and sudden cardiac death (cited in Sheps & Sheffield, 2001).

Carney and Colleagues published one of the earliest studies looking at the relationship between depression and CHD in 1987. They studied 50 patients in whom coronary angioplasty has shown evidence of CHD. Patients were assessed by the Beck Depression Inventory (Beck et al., 1961) and a semi structured interview for depression (DSM-III criteria), in addition to the State-Trait Anxiety Inventory (Spielberger et al., 1970). Twenty-six per cent of patients screened met criteria for major depression.

Univariate correlations for the presence of any cardiac event with risk factors and medications were analyzed. The strongest univariate correlations were left ventricular ejection fraction, severity of CHD, and major depressive disorder. The presence of major depressive disorder was the best single predictor of cardiac events during the first 12 months following diagnostic coronary angiography. The impact of major depressive disorder was at least equivalent to that of left ventricular dysfunction and history of previous myocardial infarction.

The presence of anxiety or depression is associated with increased reports of bothering physical symptoms, impaired social and physical function and higher death rates. E.g., the presence of clinical anxiety 48hrs after hospital admittance for Myocardial Infarction (MI) increases the complication risk 4.9 times (ischemia, infarction, and ventricular fibrillation, in - hospital death).

The presence of major depression during hospital stay increases mortality rate after stroke during the first months and the presence of subsyndromal depressive symptoms during hospital stay increases mortality after years. Anxiety worsens acute pain, and depression worsens chronic pain. A misbalance between the somatic findings and the actual level of function is a good indicator for the presence of a comorbid psychiatric disorder, most frequently anxiety or depression. Physicians regularly overlook psychiatric comorbidity, even when it impairs function.

Hospital studies clearly indicate that nurses are more able to identify psychiatric symptoms in patients compared to physicians, most likely due to their closer interaction with the patient. Relatives may also provide important information about information about change in mood and behavior, which may suggests the presence of comorbid anxiety or depression.

A decrease in heart rate variability may mediate the deleterious effect of depression on post-myocardial infarction prognosis. Other factors such as mental stress and altered platelet function may also predispose depressed patients to a heightened risk of cardiac events. With an increased understanding of the relationship between depression and heightened risk of cardiovascular mortality, it is necessary to assess current overall treatment for cardiac patients (Sheps & Sheffield, 2001). Heart disease affects an estimated 12.2 million American people. While about 1 in 20 American adults experiences major depression in a given year, the number goes to about 1 in 3 for people who have survived a heart attack. (Regier, Narrow, & Rae, 1993; Lesperance, Smith, Talajic, 1996).

Depression and anxiety disorders may affect heart rhythms, increase blood pressure, and alter blood clotting. They can also lead to elevated insulin and cholesterol levels. These risk factors, with obesity, form a group of signs and symptoms that often serve as both a predictor of and a response to heart disease. Furthermore, depression or anxiety may result in chronically elevated levels of stress hormones, such as cortisol and adrenaline. As high levels of stress hormones are signaling a "fight or flight" reaction, the body's metabolism is diverted away from the type of tissue repair needed in heart disease.

Depression is a serious medical condition that affects thoughts, feelings, and the ability to function in everyday life. Depression can occur at any age. NIMH-sponsored studies estimated that almost 10 percent of American adults, or about 19 million people age 18 and older, experience some form of depression every year. Although available therapies alleviate symptoms in over 80 percent of those treated, less than half of people with depression get the help they need (Regier, Narrow, & Rae, 1993); National Advisory Mental Health Council, 1993).

Heart disease includes two conditions called angina pectoris and acute myocardial infarction ("heart attack"). Like any muscle, the heart needs a constant supply of oxygen and nutrients that are carried to it by the blood in the coronary arteries. When the coronary arteries become narrowed or clogged and cannot supply enough blood to the heart, the result is coronary heart disease. If not enough oxygen-carrying blood reaches the heart, the heart may respond with pain called angina. The pain is usually felt in the chest or sometimes in the left arm and shoulder. (However, the same inadequate blood supply may cause no symptoms, a condition called silent angina). When the blood supply is cut off completely, the result is a heart attack. The part of the heart that does not receive oxygen begins to die, and some of the heart muscle may be permanently damaged.

Chest pain (angina) or shortness of breath may be the earliest signs of heart disease. A person may feel heaviness, tightness, pain, burning, pressure, or squeezing, usually behind the breast boned but sometimes also in the arms, neck, or jaws. These signs usually bring the person to a doctor for the first time. Nevertheless, some people have heart attacks without ever having any of these symptoms. Risk factors for heart disease other than depression include high levels of cholesterol (a fat-like substance) in the blood, high blood pressure, and smoking. On the average, each of these doubles the chance of developing heart disease. Obesity and physical inactivity are other factors that can lead to heart disease. Regular exercise, good nutrition, and smoking cessation are key to controlling the risk factors for heart disease.

Heart disease is treated in a number of ways, depending on how serious it is. For many people, heart disease is managed with lifestyle changes and medications, including beta-blockers, calcium-channel blockers, nitrates, and other classes of drugs. Others with severe heart disease may need surgery. In any case, once heart disease develops, it requires lifelong management.

Major depression is a common comorbidity associated with coronary heart disease (CHD). There is growing evidence that psychological stress in general and depression in particular predispose to cardiovascular disease. These data suggest a psychophysiologic mechanism underlying the vulnerability of depressed patients to CHD. Clinical studies have demonstrated that depression is associated with a much higher risk of both cardiovascular morbidity and mortality, which could be caused by platelet activation. Physicians should maintain a heightened level of clinical suspicion for depression and depressive disorders in persons with CHD, particularly those individuals who are recovering from myocardial infarction.

Furthermore, depression may complicate the recovery of CHD, but in most cases depression can be effectively treated with antidepressant agents (O'connor et al., 2000).

Bypass surgery and angioplasty are the most accepted techniques for curing heart diseases. Now, a growing body of research has shown that heart disease can be cured without surgery. The first evidence that lifestyle changes alone – no drugs, no surgery – can set heart disease patients on the road to improved health appeared in a study directed by Dr. Dean Ornish (1996). Based on his internationally acclaimed scientific study, which has now been ongoing for a few years, Dr. Ornish's programme has yielded amazing results.

Stress management sessions are major component of Ornish's programme. Each session is led by an instructor trained in Ornish's techniques of stress management, including stretching exercises, breathing techniques, meditation, creative visualization, and progressive relaxation. Effectively managing emotional stress not only helps eliminate one of the risk factors involved in heart disease, but also helps encourage physical, mental, and spiritual wellness.

The present investigation is intended to study the effect of similar programmes on CHD patients.

B. STATEMENT OF THE PROBLEM

The problem for the present investigation is entitled:

"EFFECT OF RELAXATION, MEDITATION, AND VISUALIZATION ON CORONARY HEART DISEASE PATIENTS".

C. HYPOTHESES

The major hypotheses formulated for the study were as follows:

1. There will be significant changes in anxiety, depression, security feeling, stress tolerance, and quality of life among coronary heart disease patients due to the intervention programme (relaxation, meditation, and visualization).

2. The intercorrelations among anxiety, depression, security feeling, stress tolerance, and quality of life will be significant.

D. METHODOLOGY IN BRIEF

(a) Sample:

A sample of sixty coronary heart disease patients was selected from PNVM Hospital at Ernakulam. The subjects were selected on the basis of the tests conducted by Cardiologist, confirming coronary heart disease. These subjects were given intervention programme.

A control group of sixty coronary heart disease patients who were not given intervention programme were also selected for comparative purposes. The age range of both the groups varied between 30 and 55 years. Both the groups were given routine medicines by the Cardiologist.

(b) Variables:

The personality variables used for the study were anxiety, depression, security feeling, stress tolerance, and quality of life.

(c) Data Collection Procedure:

1. With the help of standardized psychological tests, data on relevant variables were collected from the subjects before intervention in the case of both the groups (Pre-test data). The subjects in the experimental group were given systematic training programmes on relaxation, meditation, and visualization for 10-15 days.

These subjects were informed of the importance of the programme and were asked to continue the same as a life long procedure to be followed daily without fail. The post-test data were collected after eight months of the commencement of the programme. It may be noted that the data from the control group were also taken after eight months.

2. On selected cases, qualitative research techniques such as interview was conducted for obtaining adequate information from the subject, as part of case study.

(d) Statistical analysis:

The t–test , the Pearson r, and Case study were used for analysis of data.

E. ORGANIZATION OF THE REPORT

The report of the present investigation is presented in five chapters. Chapter I includes the importance of the investigation, statement of the problem, hypotheses, methodology in brief and, organization of the report. In Chapter II, the review of literature is presented. This chapter contains structure and functioning of the heart, physical causes of coronary heart disease, treatment of CHD, and studies related to anxiety, depression, and other variables on CHD. Chapter III gives a detailed account of the methodology, including, sample for the investigation, tools and variables, description of psychological tests for measuring the variables, data collection procedure, techniques of Lifestyle Modification Programme.

The analysis and discussion are presented in Chapter IV which contains single-group design: analysis and interpretation, two-group design: analysis and interpretation, correlation analysis, and case study. The last chapter contains the summary and conclusions of the investigation. The chapter also includes the resume of the investigation, test of tenability of the hypotheses, important findings, implications, limitations of the study, and suggestions for further research.

CHAPTER II

REVIEW OF LITERATURE

A. The heart and heart diseases
B. Physical causes of Coronary heart disease
C. Treatment of CHD
D. *Non-invasive diagnostic methods*
E. Studies related to anxiety, depression, and other variables on CHD

A. THE HEART AND HEART DISEASES

Heart disease is caused by narrowing of the coronary arteries that feed the heart. Like any muscle, the heart needs a constant supply of oxygen and nutrients, which are carried to it by the blood in the coronary arteries. When the coronary arteries become narrowed or clogged by cholesterol and fat deposits - a process called atherosclerosis – it cannot supply enough blood to the heart.

When these blockages become severe, the heart does not receive enough blood, and it becomes starved for the oxygen carried in the blood. If this deprivation is brief, the result is chest pain called angina; if prolonged, the part of the heart not receiving enough blood actually dies, and turns into scar tissue.

This is called a heart attack.

If the scar tissue is small, then the person may live. If a large part of the heart dies, or if the heart attack occurs in an important part of the heart (such as the pacemaker area, for example) then the person may not survive. (Similarly, blockages in an artery that leads to the brain can cause a stroke, in which part of the brain dies from lack of blood flow.)

On one level, blockages in the coronary arteries lead to chest pain and heart attacks, and blockages in the brain's arteries lead to strokes. To address this level of disease, doctors began performing coronary artery bypass surgery over twenty-five years ago as a way of bringing more blood around the blocked arteries. In this procedure, a vein is taken from the patient's leg and spliced around the obstructed artery, thereby increasing blood flow to the heart.

A more recent approach to treating closed arteries is called coronary angioplasty, in which a small balloon is inflated inside a blocked coronary artery, thereby 'squishing the blockage and widening the vessel, allowing more room for blood to flow to the heart. Coronary heart disease - the blockages in the coronary arteries and reduced blood flow to the heart-is the end product of a chain of events that occur over a lifetime.

The heart is situated in the middle of the chest, with more of it on the left side. The diagram of a human heart is given as Figure 1.

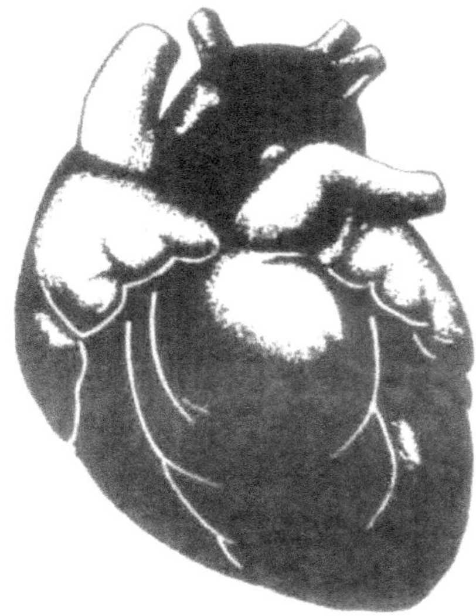

Fig . 1 . Diagram of a human heart

The heart is divided into four main chambers: each one is a bag of muscles with walls that are able to contract in order to push blood out. Each wall's thickness varies according to the amount of work it does. The walls of the left ventricle are the thickest because it does most of the pumping.

The chambers on either side of the heart are arranged in pairs. Each side has an atrium, with thin walls, to receive blood from the veins. The atrium pumps blood into a thicker walled ventricle, through which the blood is pumped into a main artery.

The heart is involved in two separate circulatory functions. Oxygen rich blood is pumped from the heart into the body through the aorta. This is called systemic circulation. When this blood is returned to the heart, after the cells have absorbed all the oxygen and nutrients, the heart pumps the blood into the lungs through the pulmonary artery. Here, the oxygen supply is replenished and the blood is returned to the heart. This is known as pulmonary circulation.

Pulmonary veins bring the newly - oxygenated blood from the lungs to the heart. It reaches the left atrium, which contracts and pushes the blood out through the mitral valve into the left ventricle. Then the left ventricle contracts. The blood moves through the open aortic valve into the aorta, and on to the system of arteries and capillaries, and into the tissues.

The deoxygenated blood from the body comes back to the heart through a large vein called the inferior vena cava, and from the head through the superior vena cava. The blood goes into the right atrium, via the tricuspid valve, and into the right ventricle. The ventricular contraction sends the blood through the pulmonic valve into the pulmonary artery, and then to the lungs. From here, the blood comes into the pulmonary veins. And the process repeats itself, about 50-60 times a minute.

Control system

The two atria contract together and fill the ventricles with blood. Then both the ventricles contract together. This is controlled by an electrical timing system located in the right atrium: the sino-atrial node. The atrioventricular node delays the electrical impulse so that the ventricles contract only after the atria.

Heart Problems and their Treatment:
Observation of Cardiological Society of India:

Common heart problems and their treatment, as presented by Cardiological Society of India are given in Table 1.

TABLE 1

Common heart problems and their treatment*

Disease/Problem	Causes	Symptoms	Treatment
Coronary artery disease	Hardening or blocking of coronary arteries with fatty deposits	Angina pain. May cause a heart attack or failure	Drugs or surgery to improve blood supply and ease pain. Diuretics to remove excess fluid from lungs and tissues.
Heart failure	A result of almost any heart disease	Breathlessness on exertion due to fluid in lungs. Swelling of ankles	Diuretics, surgery may be necessary if otherproblems, like valve disease, exist
Valve disease	Sometimes caused by rheumatic fever. Could be congenital	Same as heart failure. Angina as the heart wall thickens. Fainting when there is insufficient blood in circulation. Mitral valve problems cause palpitations	Surgery when symptoms are really bad. Otherwise, can be contained by medication. Aortic-stenosis (blocked outlet valve) needs surgery
Cardiomyopathy 1. Congestive	Cause often unknown; can be caused by alcohol, metal poisoning and hormonal conditions.	Heart failure, heart block, and palpitations. Leaky valves.	Medication, and a pacemaker, if necessary.
2. Hypertrophic	Cause unknown; may run in families	Angina and occasional fainting due to obstruction of blood flow from left ventricle	Drugs may relieve obstruction. Sometimes, an operation may be needed.
Palpitations	Anxiety and hyperactive thyroid. Abnormalities in heart structure. May occur after heart attacks.	Rapid heartbeat with dizziness or fainting due to insufficient blood supply to the brain.	Drugs to suppress abnormal heart rhythm.
Heart block (very slow heart beat)	Either a degenerative disease or as a result of heart attack.	Dizziness and fainting.	Pacemaker

*Cardiological Society of India, Kerala Chapter. (2000). Ten important advancements in cardiac care. ***The Week***, December 8, p.7.

B. PHYSICAL CAUSES OF CHD

1. MODIFIABLE RISK FACTORS

(a) Stress and Mental Tension

Psychological Stress or Tension is now recognized as the most important risk factor of coronary heart disease. Emotional stress comes in two basic categories: acute and chronic. The body responds to stress - whether emotional stress (perceived danger) or physical stress (extreme temperature changes or exertion) - by activating a series of mechanisms collectively known as the fight-or-flight response, which prepares us either to fight or to run (Chhajer, 1997).

The body does this in two ways. First, there are direct connections between your brain and your heart. These nerves, called the sympathetic nervous system, stimulate receptors in the heart that make it beat faster and harder and can cause the coronary arteries to constrict. Second, the brain causes other organs, such as adrenal glands, to secrete stress hormones such as adrenaline and steroids such as cortisol, which circulate in the blood until they reach the heart.

Acute stress tends to cause rises in production of adrenaline and noradrenaline, whereas chronic stress causes increase in cortisol (stress hormone) production. We are designed to cope with acute stress much better than with chronic stress. Unfortunately, emotional stress in modern times tends to be chronic rather than acute. The pace of life in the past ten years seems to be increasingly faster - the so-called acceleration syndrome. When our stress mechanisms are chronically activated, the same responses that are designed to protect us can become harmful - even lethal. Arteries constrict not just in our arms and legs but also inside our hearts. Blood clots are more likely to form inside our coronary arteries.

Thus, most of our muscles constrict during times of chronic, intense emotional stress, ranging from the large muscles (causing tension and pain in the neck, back, shoulders, etc.) to the smooth muscle that lines the coronary arteries (leading to spasm) to the fibres of the heart muscle itself.

Mental stress cause the heart to beat less effectively in people who had coronary heart disease. With more and more scientific research results pouring in over the last two decades, scientific literature reveal that stress can lead to the following:

1. Increase in Blood Pressure.
2. Increase in the Heart Rate.
3. Increased concentration of Fat in blood.
4. Increased Blood Sugar.
5. Increased Cholesterol in Blood.
6. Spasm of Coronary and other arteries.
7. Increased Blood Clotting.
8. Increased deposition of Fat and Cholesterol in arteries.

This means that stress is such an influential risk factor that even in the absence of other risk factors, it can by itself become responsible for coronary heart disease. People without high cholesterol, overweight, and family history, having normal blood pressure may develop angina only because of stress. It is now known that city dwellers have three times more chances of heart disease than those in small villages, the major reason being excessive stress in city life (Chhajer, 1997).

Research has also revealed that a particular type of people (Type-A behaviour) who are aggressive, always short of time, short tempered, and stressful are much more prone to develop heart disease. Most of the young heart patients of modern day have Type A behaviour (Chhajer, 1997).

It is obvious that without controlling the stresses we cannot stop the progress of heart disease. Sudden stress or anger leads to the spasm of coronary arteries which precipitates sudden angina and heart attacks. This is the reason or mechanism why many people develop heart attacks when they are excessively strained or hear a bad news.

(b) High Blood Cholesterol

Cholesterol is one of the fats which is found in the blood in free form or in combination with proteins. These combinations are called Lipoproteins.

There is a strong relationship of cholesterol in the blood and coronary heart diseases. Those people whose blood cholesterol levels are more than 200mg per cent are more prone to heart attacks than those whose levels are less than 200 mg per cent. The blood cholesterol levels are high in those people whose diet is rich in cholesterol and saturated fats, such as egg-yolk, meat, ghee, butter, cream, and cream products, and coconut oil. The range of cholesterol level in the blood is 150–200mg per cent. Blood levels more than 220mg per cent is dangerous for coronary arteries and should be immediately intervened. The previously known normal figure of 250 mg per cent is now considered very high and people are recommended to keep the blood cholesterol level lower than 200mg per cent.

The cholesterol levels in the blood can be lowered by taking a very low-fat vegetarian diet, regular physical exercise, avoiding obesity, and reducing psychological stresses. Some medicines like Lopid, Rovacor and Azstatin can artificially lower the blood cholesterol level (Chhajer, 1997). A recent report in the Journal of the American Medical Association stated that one half of all adult Americans have cholesterol levels high enough to require treatment.

(c) High Blood Triglycerides

Triglycerides are the medical term used for fat. These are very essential components of blockages and are now considered as important as cholesterol in the causation of coronary heart disease.

Triglycerides are made up of fatty acids and glycerol. These fatty acids can be saturated, mono-unsaturated or poly-unsaturated. Our food contains plenty of triglycerides. The recommended blood (serum) levels of Triglycerides are 60-130 mg per 100 ml or dl (deci litre) of blood.

(d) Low HDL (Cholesterol)

HDL (High Density Lipoprotein) cholesterol is the so called good cholesterol level, and is positively affected by lifestyle modification; including weight reduction, smoking cessation, and exercise. Even mild to moderate excess weight is associated with an increased risk of coronary heart disease. There is a consistent association between weight loss and HDL concentrations in both men and women. Weight loss consistently increases HDL concentration which is maintained as long as reduced weight is maintained. The HDL can be measured from a fasting blood sample. They have a very high affinity to bind cholesterol and can remove cholesterol from the blockages.

HDL cholesterol level in the blood should be maintained above 40 mg per 100 ml of blood to prevent heart disease. Indians are known to have low HDL cholesterol and it is often seen that the average HDL cholesterol in Indians is below 40 mg per 100 ml of blood (Chhajer, 1997).

(e) High Blood Pressure

Hypertension, or high blood pressure injures the coronary artery lining and leads to the formation of coronary blockages. When blood pressure is elevated, the blood hits the side of the arterial wall with increased force, thereby causing some injury or damage to the lining of the artery. As the artery becomes increasingly blocked, the blood pressure increases-like a garden hose whose nozzle becomes smaller and smaller. As the pressure increases, more injury to the lining occurs, causing more blockages, increasing the pressure, and so on.

The normal blood pressure in adults is between 100/60 to 140/90mm Hg. If the blood pressure is consistently more than 140/90 on two or more separate occasions, it is called ***High Blood Pressure or Hypertension***. It is a very common disease and about 20 to 30 percent of adults suffer from hypertension all over the world, but a majority of people are not even aware that they have this disease because it does not produce any symptoms in a vast number of them. That is why this disease has been correctly called the "Silent killer". High blood pressure puts an extra strain on the heart and the arteries supplying the other organs of the body.

Many diseases are caused by high blood pressure such as heart-attacks, heart–failure, kidney-failure, stroke (damage to the brain), and damage to the eyes. Higher the blood pressure, greater are the chances of getting the above diseases, mainly heart attacks.

High blood pressure can be classified as Mild, Moderate, and Severe. It is also one of the major causes of deposition of cholesterol and fat in the coronary arteries. It damages the endothelial lining of arteries, making them more prone to fat deposition. Besides a high intake of salt, psychological stresses are also implied as important causes of high blood pressure. At least 60 million Americans are considered to be hypertensive (that is, they have blood pressures greater than 140/90) (Kaplan, 1987).

A study by Schnall (1990), found that workers who faced high psychological demands without having much control over day-to-day decisions had three times the risk of having high blood pressure. All of these chronically stressed workers had thickened or enlarged hearts.

(f) Diabetes Mellitus

The normal levels of blood sugar in a fasting person are between 80-120 mg per cent. If the fasting level of blood sugar is more than 110 mg per cent, or after meals more than 160mg per cent, it is called ***high blood-sugar (Diabetes Mellitus).*** In diabetic patients, sugar can be detected in the urine also. Patients with diabetes have a higher chance of development of coronary blockages. They also get several other diseases like kidney-damage, as well as damage to the nerves and eyes.

Patients with diabetes are usually obese, have high blood pressure and high blood cholesterol levels, all responsible for blockages. Heart attacks occur at a younger age in severe diabetics. The symptoms of diabetes are increased thirst, increased urination, and weight loss, but in some there may be no symptoms at all. Control of diabetes is a must for heart patients. India has a very high number of diabetic patients.

(g) Obesity or Over -Weight

If the weight of a person is more than the upper limit of weight for that age and sex, he is called obese or a fat person. People who eat too much fat and do not do exercise put on weight. There are standard charts available from which one can find out whether one is obese. Obese individuals have greater chances of getting heart diseases. They have increased chances of getting high blood pressure and diabetes and thereby blockages. Obesity can be prevented by eating low caloric food, avoiding fats, avoiding too much sugar, and undertaking regular physical exercise. Heart attacks increase by 15 times for obese people as compared to lean and thin individuals (Chhajer, 1997).

(h) Sedentary Life or Lack of Physical Activity

Several studies have shown that people who do more of desk jobs, such as clerks, officers, doctors, lawyers, bankers etc. get more heart diseases than those whose professions require more of physical exertion, such as farmers, laborers, athletes, etc. People who have sedentary lifestyles and do not do regular physical exercises are prone to overweight. They also tend to get various joint and bone disorders due to inadequate blood circulation. Regular physical exercise not only prevents diseases like heart attacks but also keeps a person more fit and efficient. His lungs are stronger, the joints are healthy and his face and skin remains young. Therefore, exercise not only adds years to life but also life to years. But in this modern world activity has tremendously reduced.

(i) Smoking or Tobacco Consumption

Smoking of cigarettes, bidis, etc. causes several dangerous and lethal diseases like heart attacks, cancer of the lungs, bronchitis, and heart failure, stomach ulcers, arterial narrowing, etc. Several scientific studies have shown that heart disease occurs at a much younger age. The death rates due to heart attacks are higher in smokers. The risk of the heart disease and other diseases diminish if one stops smoking.

Thus, smoking can, not only kill a person early but can also cripple him because of several other dangerous diseases. Even smoking one cigarette a day does considerable harm to the body. The risk of getting heart attacks is increased by at least four fold in persons who are smoking 15 cigarettes or more every day. Consumption of Zarda, Gutka, Khaini are equally bad. It is mandatory that heart patients should stop any kind of smoking or tobacco chewing.

(j) Intake of Alchohol

Though many western studies have shown good effects of alcohol consumption the same cannot be extrapolated in Indian circumstances. India is a temperate country and people are not in the habit of alcohol consumption like those in the west. Alcohol increases the concentration of Triglycerides in the blood which predisposes further deposits. Its intoxicating effect leads people to consume more fat and food-which also indirectly promote heart disease.

2. NON-MODIFIABLE RISK FACTORS

(a) Age

Heart attacks are most frequent between the age of 40-55 years, but it is not unusual for heart attacks to occur even below the age of 40 years. These days there are chances of confronting more and more heart patients at a younger age incidence. At lease a few patients who had heart attacks are below the age of 25 years. Heart attacks occurring at younger ages are correlated to a strong family history of high blood pressure, diabetes, high blood-cholesterol levels, and heart attacks. Heavy smokers also get heart attacks at ages below 40 years.

(b) Sex

Most of the heart patients are males though the number of females is on a steady rise. The incidence of heart attacks in females is markedly less before menopause as the hormone oestrogen protects them, the exact mechanism of this hormonal protection is yet to be clearly understood but after they attain menopause (by the age of 45 to 50), they are exposed to an equal risk of getting heart attacks as males.

At present, females are burdened with work and increased stresses both at their homes and work places, and have thus become more prone to developing heart diseases.

(c) Heredity

It has been known for a long time that several members in the same family may have heart attacks. If one of the parents has had a heart attack, then the chances of the children having heart attacks becomes two fold at a still younger age. If both the parents have a heart disease, then the chances of getting a heart attack increase to four fold in their children. Heart attacks especially occur in those families where close relatives have heart attacks at a younger age, below the age of 40 years. Heart attacks in families appear to be both genetic as well as environmental. High blood pressure and diabetes which cause heart attacks are also known to be genetically determined.

It is obvious that one cannot change one's parents; so if one reduces the other risk factors of heart diseases the hereditary factor can be neutralized to a considerable extent.

Coronary Heart Disease can present itself in various ways ranging from mild chest discomfort to a heart attack or even sudden cardiac death. Whatever the presentation is, once the disease sets in, it relentlessly progresses unless preventive methods are employed to check its course. Epidemiological studies have been conducted on heart diseases in India and other developing countries of the Third World. In accordance with the latest reports, more than 13.7 per cent of the adult population is suffering from coronary heart disease in India, and this figure is constantly on the rise year after year (Chhajer, 1997).

C. THE TREATMENT OF CORONARY HEART DISEASE

The management of Coronary Heart Disease is classified according to its different methods and is further dealt in detail.

1. Medical Management

Till recently, coronary heart diseases are being treated with drugs (medicines) which result only in a temporary relief of symptoms. They under no circumstances bring about a permanent cure, as the cholesterol blockages in the coronary blood vessels are left unaffected; in other words, they act only to maintain the diseased conditions. These effects last only till the drug is in effective concentration in the blood, and gradually this concentration falls and the dose is required to be repeated.

This is a problem with the medical treatment as patients feel that they have improved and remains ignorant of the simple fact that these blockages continue to keep on gradually increasing in size as the rate of cholesterol deposition is not affected.

Most of the drugs employed in the treatment of coronary artery diseases bring about their temporary relief of symptoms through one of the following actions:

a. Vasodilators:

Some medicines dilate the coronary blood vessels, thus, increasing their luminal size and bringing about an increase of blood flow through them. These drugs have duration of action amounting to only a few hours, and after that, the coronary blood vessels once again attain their normal size by shrinking. In order to maintain the dilation, another tablet has to be taken.

b. Blood Thinning Drugs:

These drugs reduce the viscosity of blood; in other words they thin blood. Thus, through this action, more blood, which is thinned, is able to pass through the narrow space between the blockages.

c. Drugs which reduce the oxygen demand of the heart:

There is a further group of medicines which decreases the oxygen demand of the heart; thus, enabling the heart to do more work in the compromised amount of blood it is receiving due to the blocks.

d. Anti-Cholesterol Drugs:

These drugs prevent the release of triglycerides in the blood, lowering its level. The effect of these drugs is only till the drug is being taken and the fall in the blood triglyceride level is not permanent.

Nearly all the drugs used by cardiologists to treat coronary heart disease are selected from one of the above groups, and from the understanding of their mode of action, it is appreciable that all of them bring about a temporary relief from the symptoms, leaving the block as it is. In fact, they add considerably to the disease by their side-effects. When the disease process goes on gradually increasing, the medication is consequently increased with no cure. Soon, the rosy picture fades away, and one finds oneself back to where one had started from, and one realizes that everything one had gone through was all in vain.

2. Surgical Management

Over the past few decades surgery has held a key position in the management of coronary heart disease.

The surgical management of coronary heart disease involves two widely performed procedures Percutaneous Transluminal Coronary Angioplasty and Coronary Artery Bypass Grafting. These procedures have been popular and give dramatic and immediate relief from angina. This euphoria is gradually diminishing as time passes by. There are further explained below in more detail.

(a) Percutaneous Transluminal Coronary Angioplasty (PTCA):

When one or at the most two coronary arteries have significant blockages which are constantly impeding the blood flow to the heart and the patient presents with the symptoms of angina such as chest pain which may radiate to the arms, tightness in the chest, choking in the neck or breathlessness to name a few, then this procedure is generally preferred.

In this procedure, a catheter is introduced under local anesthesia either through a blood vessel in front of the elbow (brachial approach) or through a blood vessel at the loin (femoral approach). This is then guided into the heart under radiographic observation and placed at the mouth of the coronary arteries. From within this catheter another balloon tipped guide wire is introduced and the balloon is positioned at the site of the atheromatous (cholesterol containing) block. The position of the balloon is confirmed by a contrast angiography. Then the balloon is inflated a few times in order to press the block into the sides of the coronary artery and achieve a wider lumen through which more blood can pass, under angiographic observation. Then the catheters are withdrawn.

It is now a practice to insert a spring or a stent at the site of the ballooning to keep the blockages from collapsing into the lumen of the coronary artery. The patient is then kept under observation to see whether the dilated segment remains stable.

For this procedure hospital admission is necessary and the patient has to undergo various investigations and is also put on medication to facilitate the procedure.

As complicated and expensive this highly invasive procedure is, there still lies the fact that PTCA is not without serious drawbacks, and is not a permanent procedure as the block remains unremovable and the continuous deposition of cholesterol in the coronary arteries is left unarrested, and reblockages are extremely common and occurs within 3 to 6 months. Newer methods of Angioplasties such as stenting, Laser Angioplasty, Directional Atherectomy or Rota-blading do not hold the tremendous advantages which they were claimed to have. The basic process of reblockages is again related to wrong lifestyle and damaged intima of blood vessels. For reference, some of the complications of PTCA are mentioned below:

1. Injury to the coronary arteries
2. Bleeding at the site of ballooning
3. Coronary artery tear
4. Formation of out-pouchings (aneurysms) in the weakened walls of the coronary arteries
5. Sudden closure of the artery leading to a heart attack
6. New clot formation (thrombus) in the coronary artery
7. Heart attack
8. Irregular heart beats (Ventricular fibrillation)
9. Sudden cardiac arrest
10. Complications from the dye that is used for angiography still remains and is dealt elsewhere.

(b) Coronary Artery Bypass Grafting (CABG):

CABG popularly known as Bypass Surgery is another expensive surgical procedure which is a more extensive, mutilating and aggressive process of temporary solution to coronary artery disease. In this operation the chest is opened from the center in front. Blood vessels from the leg are surgically removed and used to bypass the coronary arteries which have cholesterol deposits (blockages) in them. In males, as there are no breasts an artery of the chest is available (internal mammary artery) which may be also used in the operation.

The operation is extremely complicated and intricate, and being so is not exempt from serious and fatal outcomes. The heart's function is maintained by a sophisticated machine known as a Heart Lung Machine. The procedure is left marked by a huge angry scar running down the front of the chest, and one on the leg. Although, with the help of this procedure it is possible to bypass the blockages in the main coronary arteries and their major branches, there is by no means one can operate on the smaller branches of the coronary arteries which also go to contribute extensively to the reduced supply of blood and oxygen to the muscles of the heart.

Definitely Bypass Surgery is an abnormal procedure and cannot be an exact replacement of the original. The reblockages would again occur within a gap of 2 to 12 years with an average of 5 years. Those who don't follow a proper lifestyle can even get a reblockage within 1 year, but some following a very good lifestyle would not get a reblockage for even 15 years.

Complications of CABG:

1. Respiratory complications – alveolar dysfunction, pulmonary oedema, infection, phrenic nerve injury, prolonged ventilatory insufficiency
2. Post operative hypertension
3. Heart attack (Myocardial infarction) during operation
4. Cardiogenic shock
5. Left ventricular failure
6. Cardiac tamponade
7. Septic shock

8. Arrhythmias – atrial fibrillation, atrial flutter, ventricular fibrillation
9. Blood clotting disorders
10. Wound infection, non-healing of wound
11. Peripheral vascular complications
12. Renal failure
13. Gastrointestinal complications – bleeding in the stomach, duodenum, shock liver syndrome
14. Reblockages.

D. NON–INVASIVE DIAGNOSTIC METHODS

(a) *Stress Electrocardiography (ECG)*

ECG or electrocardiogram has become a part of every cardiac evaluation. First developed in 1903, it traces on paper the pattern of heartbeats conveyed by electrodes placed on the patient's chest. Since a normal ECG at rest may not always show coronary artery disease, it is necessary to examine the adequacy of blood flow during times of increased need, say, in times of physical exertion. For this, the patient's ECG is done while he walks on a treadmill.

(b) Echocardiography

Echocardiography uses ultrasound to provide an insight into the structure and functions of the heart. It is complementary to ECG as a method of evaluation. Used in identifying coronary artery disease, it helps evaluate the extent of the disease by measuring the thickness of the left ventricular wall.

An ultrasound examination can help us see blood flow across the heart valves and the structure of the valves. It is also useful in assessing the condition of the valves.

(c) Nuclear scans

Nuclear cardiology involves using radioactive tracers to assess the condition of coronary blood flow. The functioning of the heart at rest and during exertion can be studied effectively using this method. For imaging with a radioactive agent, say, Thallium, the patient is given injections during exercise and rest.

(d) Magnetic resonance imaging (MRI)

MRI of the heart and blood vessels is under development. Excellent life like pictures of the heart and its structures are possible with an MRI.

E. STUDIES RELATED TO ANXIETY, DEPRESSION, AND OTHER VARIABLES ON CORONARY HEART DISEASE PATIENTS

The study conducted by Schleifer et al. (1989) investigated 283 patients admitted to cardiac care units for myocardial infarction at two urban hospitals. The patients were interviewed 8 to 10 days after infarction and 171 were re interviewed three to four months later. Initially, 45 per cent met diagnostic criteria for minor or major depression, including 18 per cent with major depressive syndromes.

Depression was not associated with the severity of cardiac illness but was associated with the presence of noncardiac medical illnesses. Three to four months after infarction, 33 per cent of patients met criteria for minor or major depression. The large majority of patients who initially met criteria for major but not minor depression showed evidence of depression at three months and most patients with major depression had not returned to work by three months. Treatment of major depressive syndromes may be similar to normal grief and tend to be self-limited.

In their investigation to assess the symptoms of anxiety and depression in hospitalized patients who had acute myocardial infarction (AMI); Crowe, Runions, Ebbesen, Oldridge and Streiner (1996) used State-Trait Anxiety Inventory and the short form of the Beck Depression Inventory for collecting data. The results indicated that when the patients were in the hospital the mean state4 (S-anxiety) and trait (T-anxiety) scores were 43 and 44, respectively. Ten per cent had S-anxiety scores and 14 per cent had T-anxiety scores were both 48 in-hospital, and decreased to 42 and 46, respectively, by 14 weeks and remained at these levels for the remainder of the year.

During the course of the year, 16 per cent of the patients had State-Trait Anxiety Inventory scores consistent with psychiatric conditions. The in-hospital Beck Depression Inventory mean score was 3, and 9 per cent of the patients had scores consistent with moderate to severe depression. During the first 24 weeks, symptoms of moderate to severe depression were reported by 10 per cent of the select group of patients. They concluded that the symptoms of anxiety were prevalent among hospitalized patients who had an AMI, whereas depressive symptoms were rare.

Gonzalez et al. (1996) found that depression is more prevalent in patients with coronary artery disease (CAD) than in the general elderly population. They administered structured psychiatric diagnostic interviews to 99 in-patients with CAD and diagnosed 23 per cent with a major depressive episode (MDE) by DSM-IV criteria. Severity of medical illness and family history of psychopathology were indicators for increased risk for MDE. CAD patients with depression have higher mortality rates; depression is often not recognized and treated in these patients. These findings may facilitate the recognition of CAD patients at greater risk for MDE.

Jones and West (1996) showed that there were no significant differences between rehabilitation patients and controls in reported anxiety (prevalence 33 per cent) or depression (19 per cent) at six months. Rehabilitation patients reported a lower frequency of angina (median three versus four episodes a week), medication, and physical activity. At 12 months there were no differences in clinical complications, clinical sequelae, or mortality. They concluded that the rehabilitation programmes based on psychological therapy, counselling, relaxation training, and stress management seem to offer little objective benefit to patients who have experienced myocardial infarction compared with previous reports of smaller trials.

The study conducted by Majeed and Cook (1996) concluded that, women with ischemic heart disease are as likely as men to be admitted to hospital, but after admission are less likely to undergo further investigation and revascularisation treatment. Elderly patients with ischemic heart disease are less likely than younger patients to be admitted to hospital; after admission, they are also less likely to undergo further investigation and revascularisation treatment.

Blumenthal et al. (1997) examined the extent to which ischemia induced by mental stress can be modified by exercise stress management. Their results reported that twenty-two patients (21%) experienced at least one cardiac event during a follow-up period of 21-55 months. Stress management was associated with a relative risk of 0.26 compared with controls. The relative risk for the exercise group also was lower than that of controls, but the effect did not reach statistical significance. Their result suggested that behavioural interventions offer additional benefit over and above usual medical care in cardiac patients with evidence of myocardial ischemia.

Chiou, Potempa, and Buschmann (1997) investigated the relationship among anxiety, depression, and coping methods reported by myocardial infarction (MI) patients (N=40) in Taiwan. A subset of 15 patients had high levels of anxiety and depression; however, most patients displayed low levels of anxiety and depression. A significant, moderately positive relationship was found between anxiety and the use of coping styles. An association between depression and coping styles was not found. Emotional reactions and coping methods were related to age, social class, and actual or perceived severity of MI. Their results suggested a further support for the need to evaluate the presence, intensity and influencing factors of anxiety and depression in recovery phase of MI.

The association between depressive disorders and coronary artery disease is studied by Dwight and Stoudemire (1997) who used systematic epidemiologic cirteria to examine the strength of this association. There is convincing evidence that in patients with coronary artery disease, depressive disorders are common and are associated with increased rates of morbidity and mortality. Several biological mechanisms have been proposed to explain the association, including alterations in autonomic function leading to increased risk of ventricular arrhythmias. Despite the evidence that their comorbid presence is associated with increased morbidity and mortality, depressive disorders in patients with coronary artery disease are often under diagnosed and inadequately treated. At the very least, randomized treatment trials are indicated.

Pochard, Bellivier, Faessel, and Squara (1997) describe the incidence and the prevalence of anxiety and depression, first in coronary heart disease and secondly before cardiac surgery. The prognostic significance of these psychological factors is also reviewed. Physiopathological hypothesis and practical application in clinical practice are proposed. According to the authors, previous studies have demonstrated that myocardial ischemia can be elicited by mental stress in the laboratory and during daily life and that ischemia induced by mental stress is associated with an increased risk for future cardiac events in patients with coronary artery disease.

Sarantidis et al. (1997) studied the changes in anxiety, depression from admission to discharge in patients admitted to the intensive care unit following an acute myocardial infarction. Their results indicated that the levels of both anxiety and depression increased from admission to discharge.

Hippisley-Cox, Fielding, and Pringle (1998) showed that the risk of ischemic heart disease was three times higher among men with a recorded diagnosis of depression than among controls of the same age. This association persisted when smoking status, diabetes, hypertension, and underprivileged area score were included in a multivariate model. Men with depression within the preceding 10 years were three times more likely to develop ischemic heart disease than were the controls (3.13; 1.27 to 7.70; P=0.01). Men with ischemic heart disease had a higher risk of subsequent depression than men without ischemic heart disease. Depression was not a risk factor for ischemic heart disease in women on multivariate analysis. They concluded that the depression might be an independent risk factor for ischemic heart disease in men, but not in women.

In an article Musselman, Evans, and Nemeroff (1998) review the burgeoning literature on the relationship of mood disorders and heart disease. Major depression and depressive symptoms, although commonly encountered in medical populations, are frequently underdiagnosed and undertreated in patients with cardiovascular disease (CVD). Studies investigating pathophysiological alterations related to CVD in depressed patients are reviewed. The few studies on treatment of depression in patients with CVD are also described. Treatment of depression in patients with CVD improves their dysphoria and other signs and symptoms of depression, improves quality of life, and perhaps even increases longevity. Recommendations for future research are proposed.

According to Carney, Freedland, Veith, and Jaffe (1999) effective treatments for depression are available, but unless they also improve the underlying pathophysiological or behavioral mechanisms that contribute to cardiac morbidity and mortality, they may not have beneficial effects on prognosis. Altered cardiac autonomic tone is one of the leading candidate mechanisms. Unfortunately, a review of the available research reveals that cardiac autonomic tone often fails to normalize in patients treated for depression, and the research suggests that currently available treatments for depression will not necessarily improve cardiac event free survival in patients who have had an acute myocardial infarction. Until there is convincing evidence that treatment can reduce the risk of cardiac morbidity and mortality, the principal reason to treat depression should continue to be to improve the quality of life of the patient who has had an acute myocardial infarction.

In a study on the impact of depressive symptoms and social support on 2 – year sudden cardiac death (SCD) risk, controlling for fatigue symptoms, Irvine et al. (1999) concluded that the symptoms of depression and fatigue overlap in patients with MI. The trend for the cognitive affective symptoms of depression to be associated with SCD risk, even after controlling for dyspnea/fatigue, suggests that the association between depression and mortality after AMI cannot be entirely explained as a confound of cardiac-related fatigue. The independent contribution of social participation suggests a role of both depressive symptomatology and social factors in influencing mortality risk after MI.

Recent evidence suggests that the association between depression and increased cardiac mortality may in part be due to an increase in platelet activity and an imbalance in sympathetic and parasympathetic activity that makes the patient more susceptible to ventricular fibrillation. Roose and Spatz (1999) suggest that the tricyclic antidepressants (TCAs) may increase the risk of mortality in patients with ischemic heart disease. Three studies with the selective serotonin reuptake inhibitors (SSRIs), including a double-blind, randomized comparison of paroxetine with nortriptyline, support the conclusion that the SSRIs have a relatively benign cardiovascular profile. Therefore, they are preferable to the TCAs for treatment of depression in patients at risk for cardiac events. They believed that additional studies are needed to definitively establish the cardiovascular safety of the SSRIs.

Several research findings support the proposed connection between such psychological characteristics as stress and hostility and the manifestation of disease. However, less evidence is available concerning the role(s) psychological factors might play in the process of disease recovery. Rutledge, Linden, and Davies (1999) investigated Psychological risk factors may moderate pharmacological treatment effects among ischemic heart disease patients.

Their results showed that the combination treatment produced highly significant benefits across all measured cardiac variables (20.3% improvement in exercise performance, 13% reduction in reported angina, 64.0% reduction in the frequency of: ischemic episodes; for all, $p < .01$). However, results showed that high baseline levels of daily stress were associated with reliably smaller treatment effects on measures of ischemia frequency and treadmill exorcise time and with a *significantly greater likelihood of reporting angina after treatment* ($r = -0.24, -0.25$, and -0.33, respectively; $p < .05$).

In addition, high baseline hostility predicted significantly smaller diastolic blood pressure improvements ($r = -0.29$, $p < .05$). Their results indicate that psychological risk factors may have globally negative effects on the course of treatment and suggest particular factors that may warrant attention in trials targeting cardiac symptom reduction.

Seiner and Mallya (1999) examined the evidence for cardiovascular effects of depression, as well as the proposed mechanism for these effects. Their results reported the cardiovascular effects of antidepressant treatments and the mood-altering effects of common cardiovascular medications.

Skykes, Hanley, Boyle, Higginson, and Wilson (1999) assessed the adjustment achieved by patients following discharge from coronary care and the role of socioeconomic status (SES), social environment (SE), and depression in achieving that adjustment. Two hundred eighty-seven patients were enrolled. The SE into which the patients were to be discharged was rated significantly poorer for patients of lower SES, who also scored higher on depression. At 1, 6, and 12 months post discharge, lower SES patients recorded significantly poorer levels of adjustment across a range of functioning.

Predischarge depression, together with measurers of SE and SES, determined 10 per cent to 28 per cent of the variance in 12-month post discharge adjustment. Their results suggest the importance of identifying patients at greater risk for less than optimal outcome (those lower in SES and higher in depression), and the need to address the nature of the SE in which the patient has to affect his/her recovery.

Smith and Frohm (1999) examined gender differences in the impact of depression on 1-year cardiac mortality in patients hospitalized for an acute myocardial infarction (MI). Their result shows that the depression in hospital after MI is a significant predictor of 1-year cardiac mortality for women as well as for men, and its impact is largely independent of other post-MI risks. The study conducted by Sullivan, LaCroix, Russo, Swords, Sornson and Katon (1999) determined the threshold at which depression becomes important for the daily functioning of patients with heart disease. They concluded that the patients with major depression (N=19) and patients with minor depression (N=28) were significantly more functionally impaired at baseline and at 1-year follow-up than those with no depression (N=110). The major and minor depression groups did not differ significantly.

The study conducted by Westin, Carlsson, Erhardt, Cantor-Graae and Mc Neil (1999) in Sweden in 1989-1992 to evaluate differences in quality of life (QOL) in consecutive male and female patients after acute myocardial infarction (AMI), coronary artery by-pass grafting (CABG) and percutaneous transitional coronary angioplasty (PTCA).

Somatic and psychological dimensions of QOL were assessed by self-administered questionnaire in patients one month (N=376) and one year (N=349) after the cardiac event. Normal controls (N=89) were used for comparison. Differences between gender groups, as well as between study patients and controls in somatic and psychological dimensions of QOL were studied. Patients were shown to experience poorer QOL when compared with demographically similar controls, especially at the one-month assessment.

Female patients had poorer QOL after one month (in general health, feeling of arrhythmia, anxiety, depression, self-esteem, experience of sex life) and after one year (general health, anxiety, and depression) compared with male patients. In all dimensions of QOL a proportion of patients (19 to 45%) experienced a decrease in QOL from the one-month to the one-year assessment occasion. From these findings they suggested that healthcare workers concerned with secondary prevention must be aware that QOL differs between male and female patients in several dimensions after a cardiac event. A necessary step should be taken into account in the clinical management of patients, particularly for female patients who may need special attention.

Arendarczyk and Loboz-Grudzien (2000) assessed the quality of life (QOL) and factors influencing QOL in patients 2 years after myocardial infarction. The study was performed in 100 patients with mean age 45.5, 2 years. The control group consisted of 100 healthy persons (mean age 53.5). The QOL index was assessed with the use of 2 types of questionnaires: "Quality of Well-Being Scale" (QWB) and questionnaires of QOL including 26 factors in terms of: pain, dyspnoea, anxiety, depression, energy, sleep, emotions, mobility, social isolation, sexual activity, hobby, subjective emotional, distress, functional and social state and return to work. The QOL index was assessed using mathematical Krefft method.

The result showed that the average value of QOL index in patients was significantly lower when compared with control group. The mathematical method of Ktrefft showed that out of 26 features the most important diagnostic power factor for the QOL index was: self-estimation of physical performance, return to work, the lifestyle and presence of structural pain and dyspnoea.

Social relationships and negative life events with major depression among 335 in-patients with coronary artery disease, who were free of neurological illnesses, were studied by Bosworth et al. (2000).

Depression was assessed using the Duke Depression Evaluation Schedule, a structured psychiatric interview which included the Diagnostic Interview Schedule depression sub-scale, two scales for measuring instrumental and self-maintenance activities of daily living, a measure of negative events and four dimensions of social support.

Twenty-seven subjects met DSM-IV criteria for major depression. Examination of the bivariate relationships indicated that several aspects were related to an increased likelihood of being depressed. These are: being younger, having at least one problem with an ADL and/or one IADL, being non-white, experiencing a greater number of negative events, lack of perceived social support and a lack of social interactions

In multivariate analysis depressed subjects were significantly more likely to report a greater number of negative events than non-depressed individuals after adjusting for socio demographic and ADL measures. A lack of perceived social support and increased number of negative events increased the likelihood of reporting major depressive symptoms among CAD patients. Understanding the causes of depression in CAD patients may have clinical utility in that reduction in depression may lead to a decreased risk of future CAD events.

The aim of the study conducted by Carney et al. (2000) was to determine whether treatment for depression with cognitive behaviour therapy (CBT) is associated with decreased heart rate or increased HRV. Their results suggested that treating depression with CBT may reduce heart rate and increase short-term HRV. CBT may have a beneficial effect on a risk factor for mortality in depressed patients with coronary heart disease.

Fraguas, Ramadan, Pereira, and Wajngarten (2000) investigated the determinants and maintain factors of depression in patients undergoing coronary artery bypass graft (CABG). Fifty CABG candidates were selected randomly for evaluation before and after surgery. Depressive disorders occurred in 22.0 per cent of the patients preoperatively and 21 per cent postoperatively. Irritability as a symptom was more prevalent in depressed than nondepressed patients preoperatively (P=.04) and postoperatively (P=.006).

Although depression was the most prevalent diagnosis in the patients' psychiatric histories and evaluations, benzodiazepines were prescribed more frequently than antidepressants (70% vs 3%). They suggested that Cardiologists should consider that the irritability in some patients undergoing CABG might obscure the diagnosis of depression. The correct recognition of depression is essential to reduce inappropriate benzodiazepine prescription and to apply appropriate treatment.

The association between depression and anxiety and recurrent coronary heart disease events during the first 12 months subsequent to myocardial infarction, was studied by Janne et al. (2000). The Beck Depression Inventory and the State-Trait Anxiety Inventory were completed during hospitalization by 288 myocardial infarction patients. Peel index score and Killip class were used as indices of disease severity. The 12month incidence of recurrent coronary heart disease events (fatal and non-fatal) was determined. Eighty-two patients experienced recurrent coronary heart disease events, including 27 cardiac fatalities, during follow-up.

Whereas the Peel Index differentiated patients who experienced recurrent events from those who did not symptoms of depression and anxiety were unrelated to outcome. They concluded that depression and anxiety did not predict subsequent coronary heart disease events and were not associated with either Peel Index scores or Killip class.

In this article Ketterer, Mahr, and Goldberg (2000) reviews the nature of the scientific evidence necessary to accept an etiological or aggravating role for psychological events. It has been pointed out that with the increase in well-designed and carefully executed epidemiological and treatment studies, this diagnostic category has evolved into an arena where cutting edge insights and therapies are becoming available for a growing variety of medical conditions, especially coronary heart disease.

Epidemiological research over the past decade indicated that major depression and depressive symptomatology are common among patients with coronary heart disease (CHD) and postmyocardial infarction. Major depression is a serious, debilitating comorbid disorder that can significantly increase risk for and complicate recovery from cardiac events (e.g., myocardial infarction). Unfortunately, major depression is rarely detected or treated in the cardiology setting. However, it is a disorder that can be successfully and safely treated in the majority of cases.

Although the mechanisms that may be mediating the depression – CAD link are less well understood, there are several plausible mechanisms by which depression may influence the course and outcome of CAD. This review by Lavoie and Fleet (2000) examined the literature linking major depression and depressive symptomatology to CAD course and outcome, and makes recommendations for improving assessment and treatment of depression in the cardiology setting.

Some degree of depression affects at least 30 per cent of hospitalized patients with coronary artery disease (CAD), and is associated with increased risks of mortality and continuing depression over at least the first year following hospital discharge. Despite its consequences for prognosis and quality of life, depression is under recognized and under treated in cardiac patients. The diagnosis of depression is complicated in patients with medical illness. Their symptoms can reflect physical as well as psychological complaints.

Many CAD patients resist the idea of additional medications, and drug interactions can be problematic for those willing to accept antidepressant treatment. Finally, depression tends to recur. Its successful treatment requires a long-term commitment from both physician and patient. Lesperance and Smith (2000) examined the special challenges involved in diagnosing depression in patients with CAD. They outline available psychotherapeutic and pharmacological treatments, and consider the issues involved in deciding which patients to treat, with what approach, and for how long.

Malhotra, Tesar, and Granco (2000) point out that the expanding scientific evidence supports a long-recognized link between cardiovascular disease and depression. As an independent risk factor, depression increases patient vulnerability to both cardiac events and mortality. Several important pathophysiologic mechanisms have been proposed, including hypothalamic-pituitary axis hyperactivity, autonomic nervous system dysfunction, and increased platelet reactivity, among others. The recently completed Sertralie Antidepressant Heart

Attach Randomized Trial inaugurates a series of studies intended to address the impact of antidepressant therapy on cardiovascular risk.

Mayou et al. (2000) investigated the significance of emotional distress immediately after a myocardial infarction as a predictor of physical, psychological, and social outcomes and resource use. The results showed that fifteen per cent of patients scored as probable cases of anxiety or depression. They were likely to report pre infarct distress and poor adjustment. There was an improvement at 3 months, but there was little overall or individual change after that time. Anxiety and depression did not predict subsequent mortality but did significantly predict poor outcome at 1 year on all dimensions of the 36-item short form quality-of-life measure and on specific measures of everyday activity and reports of chest pain, use of primary care resources, and secondary prevention lifestyle changes.

They concluded that the subjects who are distressed in the hospital are at high risk of adverse psychological and quality-of-life outcomes during the ensuing year. Their findings strengthen the argument for in-hospital identification and treatment of patients with depression and anxiety after myocardial infarction.

O'connor, Gurbel, and Serebruany (2000) observe that persons who have mental stress during daily life are at twice the risk of CHD, and patients with post-myocardial infarction depression have higher mortality rates than nondepressed controls. These data suggest a psychophysiologic mechanism underlying the vulnerability of depressed patients to CHD. Clinical studies have demonstrated that depression is associated with a much higher risk of both cardiovascular morbidity and mortality, which could be caused by platelet activation. Physicians should maintain a heightened level of clinical suspicion for depression and depressive disorders in persons with CHD, particularly those individuals who are recovering from an acute myocardial infarction. Furthermore, depression may complicate the recovery of IHD, but in most cases depression can be effectively treated with antidepressant agent.

Smith and Frohm (2000) investigated depression in the hospital after myocardial infarction (MI) has been associated with a substantial increase in the long term risk of cardiac mortality, but little is known about other outcomes. Their results showed that the total costs (outpatient physician charges plus physician costs during admissions plus estimates of associated direct costs), were about 41 per cent higher (p=0.004) for patients with elevated BDI scores. The difference was primarily related to out-patient and emergency room visits and readmission costs associated with longer stays in hospital wards, and were not accounted for by use of psychiatric services or readmissions for revascularization.

Their results suggest in addition to the survival risks associated with post-MI depresssion, there are increased health care costs linked to both readmissions and outpatient contacts among depressed patients who survive the first post-MI year. The extent to which the increased use of health care may have reduced depression and enhanced survival remains unclear.

Stein et al. (2000) examined the relationship between depression and heart rate variability (HRV) in cardiac patients. They revealed that the association of moderate to severe depression with reduced HRV in patients with stable CHD may reflect altered cardiac autonomic modulation and may explain their increased risk for mortality.

Fruthwald et al. (2001) assessed the prevalence of anxiety disorders and depression is between 20 and 50 per cent following stroke. Depressive persons tend to give their overall life situation a worse rating than their relatives or physicians because of negative cognitions. Nevertheless, research concerning Quality of Life (QOL) after stroke hardly ever takes into accounts the methodological bias of assessing (QOL) only by self-rating.

The aim of the study was to point out the important relationship between depression, anxiety and the auto assessment of QOL. QOL was markedly affected in the post stroke patients and in the chronic low back pain and myocardial ischemia patients and it was rated worst by the most seriously depressed subjects. Clinical studies focusing on the ever more significant evaluation criterion "health-related QOL" after stroke should take into account the high prevalence of anxiety and depressive symptoms and their major influence on the patient's self-evaluated QOL.

Lane et al. (2001) investigated the impact of symptoms of depression and anxiety on mortality and QOL in 288 patients hospitalized for acute myocardial infarction (MI). The study reported that the symptoms of depression and anxiety did not predict either cardiac or all-cause mortality after MI, but they did predict QOL among those who lived to 12 months.

Penninx et al. (2001) showed that depression increases the risk for cardiac mortality in subjects with and without cardiac disease at baseline. The excess cardiac mortality risk was more than twice as high for major depresssion as for minor depression. Suadicani, Hein and Gyntelberg (2001) conducted a study to elucidate the role of socio-economic status as a risk factor for CHD mortality in middle-aged men. They concluded that the risk factors with an uneven social distribution related to occupation and lifestyle were strong mediators of the association of socioeconomic status with risk of IHD. A quite strong explanatory potential persisted but diminished with length of follow-up.

Sullivan, La Croix, Russo, and Walker (2001) revealed that the effect of depression on self-reported physical health is significantly mediated by physical symptoms (angina and fatigue), personality states and traits (positive affect and novelty seeking), and spousal support. Positive affect and novelty seeking had more marked effects on physical health in the presence of more depression. A broad range of factors beyond the severity of coronary disease itself affects the perceived physical health of patients with CHD.

Bokhari et al. (2002) examined the prevalence of depression in patients CAD in a tertiary care hospital setting in Pakistan. Their sample consisted of 154 patients of CAD (115 males and 39 females) who were randomly selected from the outpatient department and wards of the National Institute of Cardiovascular Diseases, Karachi and was scored for depression via the Hospital Anxiety and Depression Scale.

The results indicated that the point prevalence of depression in the sample was 37% (31.3% males and 53.8% females). Female sex, income level below Rs.5000 per month, low education level, outpatient, single earning family member and hypertension were few variables associated positively with depression ($p<0.05$). They concluded that depression is prevalent in CAD patients in Pakistan. Economic conditions may pose an additional threat on these patients. The physicians (especially cardiologists) need to be aware of this co-morbidity so as to be able to diagnose and adequately manage such patients.

The study by Jastrebow et al. (2002) indicated that 30 percent of cardiac, 39 per cent of orthopedic and 81 per cent of psychosomatic patients have symptoms of anxiety and/or depression.

Lane et al. (2002) assessed the prevalence and persistence of symptoms of depression and anxiety during the first 12 months following acute myocardial infarction (MI). In a prospective study, 288 MI patients were assessed for symptoms of depression and anxiety using the Beck Depression Inventory (BDI) and the State-Trait Anxiety Inventory (STAI) in hospital, 2-15 days following MI, and 4 and 12 months subsequently.

Results showed that during hospitalization, 89 (30.9%) and 75 (26.1%) patients registered elevated BDI scores and state anxiety scores (greater than or equal to 40), respectively. The 4 and 12-month prevalence rates were 37.7 per cent and 37.2 per cent for depressive symptoms, and 41.8 per cent and 40.0 per cent for anxious symptoms, respectively. They concluded that the symptoms of depression and anxiety are prevalent, persistent problems during the first year following MI. This study also highlights the importance of routine psychological assessment for MI patients both in hospital and after discharge.

Romanelli, Fauerbach, Bush, and Ziegelstein (2002) studied the significance of post-MI depression in individuals aged 65 and older. They concluded that older post-Nil patients with depression have more comorbidities than older patients without depression and have almost four times the risk of dying within the first four months after discharge. Although this increased risk is likely to be related to many factors, the data suggested that sicker patients who are older and depressed may less often be prescribed medications known to reduce post-MI mortality and may also have greater difficulty following recommendations to reduce cardiac risk than their counterparts without depression. Efforts to improve adherence to post-Nil treatment guidelines and to enhance patient compliance may improve prognosis in this high-risk group.

Fenner and Michels (2003) studied 134 patients with acute myocardial infarction, who were treated in an intensive care unit (ICU) of a German hospital were selected for the study to examine their psychological symptoms. Their results indicated that the patients with a low social status were found to have elevated mean values of the following scales: somatization (0.93), depression (0.66), and anxiety (0.59). The Global Severity Index (GSI) as a global measure of psychological distress was elevated as well (0.46).

They concluded that, since patients with a limited social network and low social status, increased anxiety and depressive scores have a poor prognosis as to their mortality, and their professional reintegration, it was considered necessary for the prospective setting of this study to register particularly those patients in order to treat their anxiety.

Several studies have been conducted by previous researchers on heart diseases, on methods of treatment, and on variables and methods associated with it. Some of the relevant studies are reported below under various heads.

1. *Studies showing effect of relaxation, meditation, and visualization on coronary heart disease patients*

The studies reported in this section are related to the different techniques adapted for curing heart diseases, with emphasis on three of these, viz.,relaxation, meditation, and visualization. It may be noted here that all these studies are reported during or after 1990, though one or more of the above techniques are found reported prior to 1990 (noted elsewhere in this chapter).

Kapadia (1996) in his Universal Healing Programme (Practices relaxation, meditation, and visualization) has observed that after attending only 10 to 12 sessions over a period of 6 weeks, a majority of the participants not only reported benefit in the number of episodes of anginal pain but are also motivated to make lifestyle changes, i.e., giving up smoking, alcohol and choosing low-fat vegetarian diet. Within three months their level of hostility dropped remarkably.

In another study by Kapadia (1996) on 25 patients in the rehabilitation programmes of Universal Healing Programme, it was found that there was 22.8 per-cent increase in conditioning index; 59 per cent increase in exercise performance and decrease in medications. The conditioning index has been accepted as a reliable and quantifiable indicator of exercise tolerance achieved on Treadmill Test (TMT). It is a valuable aid in assessing the benefit achieved by the exercise training.

In 1995, data of 113 patients have been taken at random to study the feedback of the Universal Healing Programme (Kapadia, 1995). In almost all the participants, the fear of death vanished and all had become very compassionate, friendly, and co-operative in every sphere of life. All those who were advised CABG (Coronary Artery Bypass Grafting) or angioplasty, are convinced that they do not need any such interventions. They are able to control minor episodes of angina with abdominal breathing and overcome sleeplessness with relaxation technique and meditation. Some observe that visualization after meditation helps them to increase their capacity to work without angina.

A large-scale study in Helsinki compared 612 people who were intensively treated with anti-hypertensive and cholesterol-lowering drugs to a control group of 610 people who received usual medical care with fewer drugs. Although these drugs produced a 35% overall reduction in risk factors in the drug-treated group, the participants developed twice as much heart disease after five years when compared with the control group of patients that took fewer anti-hypertensive and cholesterol-lowering drugs. In patients with severe hypertension, then they will begin treating elevated blood pressure with medication while simultaneously recommending the life-style programme. Patients who follow this programme will often show significant reductions in blood pressure, and can discontinue blood pressure medications slowly as this occurs.

In their study, Song, Schwartz, and Russek (1998) examined many relaxation, meditation, and imagery techniques that implicitly or explicitly involve focused attention on the body, including qigong, massage, and non contact therapeutic touch, purportedly employ energetic physiological mechanisms the objective is to show that, from perspective of dynamical energy systems, relaxed self-attention enhances connectivity between the brain and body. This enhanced connectivity may be achieved by at least two mechanisms: (i) physiological mechanisms employing peripheral negative feedback loops, and (ii) bioelectromagnetic mechanisms involving direct energetic resonance between the peripheral organ and the brain. Nineteen channels of electroencephalogram, 1 electrocardiogram, and 2 channels of electro-oculogram were recorded from 22 subjects who focused their attention on their heartbeats or eye movements, with and without kinesthetic (touch) biofeedback to increase somatic awareness. Analysis of the electroencephalogram synchronized with the electrocardiogram revealed significant effects for heart-focused attention, primarily with touch biofeedback, following the contraction of the ventricles (possibly reflecting increased baroreceptor and somatosensory feedback); and significant effects for heart-focused attention, with and without touch biofeedback, preceding the contraction of the ventricles (possibly reflecting direct electromagnetic interactions between the heart and the brain). These findings suggest that energetic and physiological mechanisms may be involved in techniques in which the goal is to promote mind-body integration and health.

Rutledge et al. (1999) examined clinical outcomes in 71 male and female patients with coronary atherosclerosis who were enrolled in a 2-year, independent-living, lifestyle modification programme. The findings in 43 patients who completed the programme were compared with those in 28 patients who dropped out of the programme. Clinical studies suggest that lifestyle modification of risk factors for coronary atherosclerosis were managed for a two year period in a structural multidisciplinary reduces subsequent cardiac events but there are very few reports of the effect of these programmes in patients living independently.

Patients with diagnosed coronary atherosclerosis were managed for a two year period in a structured multidisciplinary programme by a team that included two cardiologists, a nurse, a dietitian, an exercise physiologist, and a clinical psychologist. The overall aim of the programme was to normalize or control all *major reversible cardiovascular risk factors.*

Patients were required to participate in several weekly sessions for exercise, meditation, stress reduction training, dietary education and counselling, and participatory dinners. There was a strong emphasis on patient's self care, inclusion of support members, and regular monitoring of and feedback to patients. The data comparing baseline and 2 - year outcomes showed a significant reduction in body weight, dietary intake of total/saturated fat and cholesterol, serum low and high density lipoprotein concentration, and an increase in exercise capacity. In the compliant group, the incidence of cardiac events was 2.3% over 2 years. Multidisciplinary lifestyle modification programmes addressing cardiovascular risk factors are known to have a significants impact upon cardiac risk factors in patients with coronary atherosclerosis. Data show that these changes can be accomplished in independent living patients in a programme offered through a routine cardiology service. However, compliance is an important issue in these self-regulated programmes.

Ornish et al. (1990) study showed that patients' blood cholesterol levels were reduced by almost 40 per cent, blood flow to the heart was improved and chest pain (angina) was reduced by 91 per cent. Ornish maintains that simple lifestyle changes – eating a low fat, vegetarian diet, incorporating a series of stress management techniques (Relaxation, Meditation, and Visualization) into the daily routine, exercising, and stopping smoking-can result in better health and an improved quality of life.

Ornish et al. (1998) examined the feasibility of patients to sustain intensive lifestyle changes for a total of five years and the effects of these lifestyle changes (without lipid-lowering drugs) on coronary heart disease. Forty-eight patients with moderate to severe coronary heart disease were randomized to an intensive lifestyle change group or to a usual-care control group, and 35 completed the 5-year follow-up quantitative coronary arteriography. Intensive lifestyle changes (10 per cent fat whole foods vegetarian diet, aerobic exercise, stress management training, smoking cessation, group psychosocial support) for five years. Experimental group patients (20 – (71 per cent) of twentyeight patients completed five year follow-up) made and maintained comprehensive lifestyle changes for five years, whereas control group patients (15 – (75 per cent) of twenty patients completed five year follow-up) made more moderate changes. In the experimental group, the average per cent diameter stenosis at baseline decreased 1.75 absolute percentage points after one year. In contrast, the average per cent diameter stenosis in the control group increased by 2.3 percentage points after one year and by 11.8 percentage points after five years. Twenty-five cardiac events occurred in 28 experimental group patients vs 45 events in 20 control group patients during the five year follow-up. More regression of coronary atherosclerosis occurred after five years than after one year in the experimental group. In contrast, in the control group, coronary atherosclerosis continued to progress and more than twice as many cardiac events occurred.

The above studies could clearly point out the positive effect of relaxation, meditation, and visualization on coronary heart disease patients.

2. *Studies showing effect of meditation and visualization on coronary heart disease patients*

The following literature indicates the effect of meditation and visualization on coronary heart disease patients. The investigators did not include relaxation in the programme.

Luskin et al. (1998) studied complementary and alternative treatments, especially mind-body techniques. The goals of the study were to establish a comprehensive literature review and to provide rationality for future research concerning successful aging. All studies since 1990 that examined mind-body treatments of cardiovascular disorders in the elderly were included. Mind-body practices evaluated were social support, cognitive-behavioural treatment, meditation, the placebo effect, faith, hope, imagery, spiritual healing, music therapy, hypnosis, yoga, t'ai chi, qigong and aikido.

Studies conducted after 1990 were a priority, but when more recent literature was scarce, other studies using randomized, controlled trials were included. Mind-body techniques were found to be efficacious primarily as complementary and sometimes as stand-alone alternative treatments for cardiovascular disease-related conditions. Studies provided evidence for treatment efficacy, but the need for further controlled research was evident. Reviewers found only a handful of randomized, controlled research studies conducted in the United States. As a result, there is a lack of replicated studies with which to determine appropriate treatment dosage and the mechanisms by which many of the practices work. Compelling anecdotal evidence, the presence of some controlled research, overall cost effectiveness, and the lack of side effects resulting from mind-body treatment make further investigation a high priority.

3. Studies showing effect of relaxation and meditation on coronary heart disease patients

The two studies reported below had used various relaxation and meditation techniques for curing heart diseases.

Travis et al. (1976) studied a group of transcendental meditators, and a group of control subjects instructed to relax, were compared with respect to degree of relaxation reached as measured by changes in heart rate, tension of the frontalis muscle, and occipital alpha production. The only significant changes were decreases in these measures over time in the control subjects. The changes in the controls were probably the consequence of sleep or the onset of sleep.

In order to study the effects of behaviour therapy, self-relaxation transcendental meditations on cardiovascular stress response, Puente and Beiman (1980) compared Behaviour Therapy (BT), self-relaxation (SR), Transcedental Meditations (TM), and a waiting-list control group (WL) on measures of cardiovascular and subjective stress response. Male and female respondents

(N=60) to an ad for therapy were evaluated in assessment sessions before and after treatment. The results indicated that BT and SR were more effective than either TM or WL in reducing cardiovascular stress response. These data were interpreted as resulting from therapeutic suggestion and positively reinforced client progress. These studies indicated that the techniques used by the investigators where of help to the patients for getting coronary heart disease cured.

4. *Study showing the effect of relaxation on CHD patients*

With an objective to investigate on trial of relaxation in reducing coronary risk, Patel, Marmot, Terry, Carruthers, Hunt (1985) screened 192 men and women aged 35-64, and were identified as having two or more of the following risk factors: blood pressure greater than or equal to 140/90 mm Hg, plasma cholesterol concentration greater than or equal to 6.3 mmol/l (243.6 mg/100 ml), and current smoking habit greater than or equal to ten cigarettes a day. They were randomly allocated to a group for modification behaviour or to serve as controls.

Both the groups were given health education leaflets containing advice to stop smoking, to reduce animal fats in the diet, and on the importance of reducing blood pressure. In addition, the treatment group had group sessions of one hour a week for eight weeks in which they were taught breathing exercises, relaxation, and meditation, and about managing stress.

It had previously been found that after eight weeks and eight months there was a significantly greater reduction in both systolic and diastolic blood pressures in the group taught to relax compared with the control group. After four years of follow up, these differences in blood pressure were maintained. Plasma cholesterol concentration and the number of cigarettes smoked were lower in the treatment group at eight weeks and eight months but not at the four years follow up. At four years, more subjects in the control group reported having had angina and treatment for hypertension and its complications. Incidence of ischaemic heart disease, fatal myocardial infarction, or electrocardiographic evidence of ischaemia was significantly greater in the control group.

The authors observed that if results of the study could be obtained in a larger study the financial and health care implications would be enormous.

5. Studies showing effect of meditation on CHD Patients

Research study indicates that meditation and transcendental meditation were subjected to study to show its effect on coronary heart disease patients.

The "Impact of Transcendental Meditation on cardiovascular function at rest and during acute stress in adolescents with high normal blood pressure", was studied by Barnes, Treiber, Davis (2001), who examined the impact of the TM a programme on cardiovascular reactivity in subjects adolescents with high normal blood pressure. This study made use of thirty five adolescents [34 African American, 1 Causacian American; ages 15 - 18 years] with resting systolic blood pressure between the 85th and 95th percentile for their age and gender on three consecutive occasions, were randomly assigned to either TM (n = 17) or health education control (n = 18) groups. The TM group engaged in 15 - min meditation twice each day for two months including session during school lunch break. Primary Cardiovascular outcome measures were changes in blood pressure, heart rate, and cardiac output at rest and in response to two laboratory stressors, a simulated car driving stressor and an inter personal social stressor interview.

This study concluded that the Transcendental Meditation programme appears to have a beneficial impact upon Cardiovascular functioning at rest and during acute laboratory stress in adolescents at risk for hypertension.

Wenneberg et al. (1997) conducted a controlled study of the effects of the Transcendental Meditation programme on cardiovascular reactivity and ambulatory blood pressure. Cardiovascular responses to stress reactivity have been proposed as a risk factor for hypertension. The investigators evaluated the effects of stress reduction on both laboratory cardiovascular reactivity and ambulatory blood pressure on 39 normontensive male subjects who were pretested for ambulatory blood pressure. Meditation technique or a cognitive-based stress education control (SEC) for four months. After four months, there was no change in cardiovascular response to stressor between the TM and control groups. However, the subjects regularly practicing Transcendental Meditation demonstrated a significant reduction of 9 mm Hg ($p < .04$) in average ambulatory DBP compared to controls. Since ambulatory BP monitoring has been shown to be a better predictor of cardiovascular complications of hypertension than clinic BP, this finding may have important implications for primary prevention of CVD in normotensive subjects.

Zamarra et al. (1996) studied twenty-one patients with documented coronary artery disease. The subjects were tested at baseline by exercise tolerance testing, and assigned to either stress reduction using the Transcendental Meditation (tm) programme or to a wait-list control. After 8 months, TM group had a 14.7 % increase in exercise tolerance, and 11.7% increase maximal workload, an 18% delay *in onset of* ST - *segment depression,* and *significant reductions in* rate-pressure product at 3 and 6 minutes, and at maximal exercise compared with the control group.

The effect of meditation training on aspects of coronary-prone behaviour was subjected to study by Muskatel, Woolfolk, Carrington, Lehrer, and McCann (1984). They studied 52 undergraduates who had volunteered to receive meditation training. The subjects were placed into either high or low time-urgency groups based on their scores on Factor S of the Jenkins Activity Survey. Subjects then either received training in Clinically Standardized Meditation followed by three and half week of practice or waited for training during that period. Analysis of scores on a time-estimation task and of self-reported hostility during an enforced waiting task indicated that meditation significantly altered subjects' perceptions of the passage of time and reduced impatience and hostility resulting from enforced waiting.

As has been stated under each of the above categories meditation itself was shown to be effective on coronary heart disease patients, as evidenced by the results of a few studies reported in this section.

6. Study showing effect of spirituality on CHD patients

It is interesting to note that spirituality is related to the treatment of coronary heart disease.

Franklin (2000) suggested that religious involvement or spiritual well-being affect health outcomes. A study was designed by the author to investigate whether the scores from a questionnaire measuring spiritual well-being correlated with progression or regression of coronary heart disease as measured with computerized cardiac catheterization data. Participants in Dr. Dean Ornish's Lifestyle Heart Trial were given the "Spiritual Orientation Inventory". A significant difference was found in the spirituality scores between a control group and a research group that practiced daily meditation. The spirituality scores were significantly correlated with the degree of progression or regression of coronary artery obstruction over a 4-year time period. The lowest scores of spiritual well-being had the most regression. This study suggested that the degree of spiritual well-being might be an important factor in the development of coronary artery disease.

7. Studies showing effect of psycho-social factors and bio-psychosocial interventions on CHD patients

Psychosocial factors and biopsychosocial intervention techniques have been considered as crucial in the case of patients with coronary heart disease. Different types of training procedures have been adapted by various investigators in different countries with a view to understand its effect on heart related problems. Most of these studies have shown that there is positive effect, as the result of practice. A few of these studies are reported below:

The study on "Effect of Qi-training on blood pressure, heart rate, and respiration rate", conducted by Lee, Kim,Huh, Ryu,Chung (2000) examined the physiological effects of Korean traditional Qi-training. They investigated the changes in blood pressure, heart and respiratory rates before, during and after ChunDoSunBup(CDSB) Qi-training. Twelve normal healthy CDSB Qi-trainees (19-37 years old; trained for 1.3+/-0.2 years; 9 men and 3 women) volunteered to participate in this study. Heart rate, respiratory rate, systolic blood pressure and rate-pressure product were significantly decreased during Qi-training. From these results, they suggested that CDSB Qi-training had physiological effects that indicated stabilization of cardiovascular system.

Pandya et al. (1999) had observed that conventional mind-body therapy has a valuable noninvasive way to manage coronary disease. Yoga practice, especially, has been found to be valuable in preventing adverse outcomes of coronary disease by improving resistance to stress.

In their study on outcomes after myocardial infarction, Buselli, Stuart (1999) has observed that psychosocial factors can adversely affect cardiac health. The author holds that Psychosocial factors such as depression, coronary-prone behaviour, hostility, social isolation, anxiety, anger, and stress are related to increased cardiac death and illness. According to him, various interventions including cognitive-behavioural therapies, techniques that elicit the relaxation response, meditation, exercise, and increasing social networks, may play a role in improving health outcomes. This article explores the relationship of these psychosocial factors to cardiac health.

Mockel et al. (1994) studied a group of 20 healthy volunteers (10 men; median age 25 (20-33) years) were examined by means of pulsed wave Doppler echocardiography, blood sample analysis, and psychological testing before and after listening to three different examples of music: a waltz by J. Strauss, a modern classic by H. W. Henze, and meditative music by R. Shankar. The mental state was measured by using a psychological score (Zerssen) with low values (minimum 0) for enthusiastic and high values (maximum 56) for depressive patterns. The mental state was improved (Zerssen: 6.5 vs 11 points ; $P < 0.05$).

In their study on Psychological treatment of cardiovascular disease, Blanchard, Miller (1977) reviewed four categories: hypertension, cardiac arrhythmias, coronary artery disease and peripheral circulatory disease. In the treatment of hypertension biofeedback of blood pressure, electromyography and galvanic skin responses both seem useful, as does systematic relaxation training of either an active or passive meditative nature. Biofeedback of heart rate had shown some utility in treating premature ventricular contractions and sinus tachycardia. Supportive and educational group therapy for patients recovering from myocardial infarctions had shown some utility;. In the treatment of Raynaud's disease, biofeedback of skin temperature is helpful. In no area has a large scale clinical trial been conducted, and only three controlled group outcome studies have been reported (two in hypertension, one in coronary artery disease).

8. Study showing effect of breathing on CHD patients

In their study on Influence of different combination of mental activity and respiratory cycle on heart rate variability, Sun, Li DM, Li GY (1996) in Beijing examined by means of spectral analysis of P-R interval, different characteristics of heart rate variability in different form of respiratory exercise was observed. The results of observation on 32 volunteers showed that mental activity that affected respiration, can influence the function of autonomic nerve system in a different way. When the mind concentrated at the inspiration, the function of autonomic nerve system was kept in balance, and both the sympathetic and the vagal activities enhanced significantly. While the mind concentrated at the expiration, a reduction of vagal activity was induced so as to produce marked change in the sympathovagal balance.

9. Study showing the effect of Alternative Medicine on CHD patients

In their study on "The state of Complementary and Alternative Medicine in Cardiovascular, Lung and Blood Research", Lin, Nahin, Gershwin, Longhurst (2001) focused on 5 areas of research, including a historical and cultural perspective of Complementary and Alternative Medicine (CAM), methodological issues in clinical trials, herbal medicine, chelation therapy, mind/body (meditation) therapy, and acupuncture. CAM has become widely used without rigorously proven efficacy and safety. To protect the public, it was recommended that the fundamental mechanistic research for these CAM approaches be vigorously pursued and that any large-scale clinical trial be carefully executed to avoid any waste of resources and any unnecessary risk. It was felt that standardization of botanical products and procedure-based CAM intervention, such as acupuncture and meditation, is essential for meaningful basic and clinical research. Although botanical products properly consumed are perceived as generally safe, potential herb-drug interactions are a major safety concern. Clearly, many challenges need to be addressed by the scientific community before the public can be assured of the proper use of CAM.

10. *Study on Meditation in healthy people*

Peng et al. (1999) reported extremely prominent heart rate oscillations associated with slow breathing during specific traditional forms of Chinese Chi and Kundalini Yoga meditation techniques in healthy young adults. They applied both spectral analysis and a novel analytic technique based on the Hilbert transform to quantify these heart rate dynamics. The amplitude of these oscillations during meditations was significantly greater than in the pre-meditation control state and also in three non-meditation control groups: i) elite athletes during sleep, ii) healthy young adults during metronomic breathing, and iii) healthy young adults during spontaneous nocturnal breathing. This finding, along with the marked variability of the beat-to-beat heart rate dynamics during such profound meditative states, challenges the notion of meditation as only an autonomically quiescent state.

Conclusions of the studies

A majority of the studies had used one or more of the techniques such as relaxation, meditation, visualization, cognitive behavioural treatment, spiritual healing, music therapy, hypnosis, yoga, t'ai chi, qigong, and aikido. The sample used in these studies varied widely, with small or large sample size. Different methods have been used to measure the conditions of the patients before and after applying the respective techniques. These studies in general provided an adequate picture for the investigator to formulate a suitable design for the present research work.

CHAPTER III

METHODOLOGY

A. Sample for the investigation
B. Tools and variables
C. Data collection procedure
D. Statistical techniques used for quantitative analysis
E. Procedure for qualitative analysis
F. Techniques of lifestyle modification programme

The methodology or plan and procedure of the present investigation has been presented below under various heads, in detail, namely,

a. Sample for the investigation

b. Tools and Variables

c. Data Collection Procedure

d. Analysis

A. SAMPLE FOR THE INVESTIGATION

The present investigation made use of a sample of sixty coronary heart disease patients selected from PNVM Hospital at Ernakulam. The subjects were selected on the basis of the tests conducted by Cardiologist, confirming coronary heart disease. These subjects were given intervention programme. A control group of sixty Coronary heart disease patients who were not undergoing intervention programme were also selected for comparative purposes.

The age range of both the groups varied between 30 and 55 years. Both the groups were given routine medicines by the Cardiologist.

Sampling

Sampling is the process of obtaining information regarding the population, examining only a part of it. Sampling means selection of a few items from a given group to be investigated in such a way as to serve data on the basis of which responsible conclusions can be drawn regarding the population. The basic objective of sampling is to obtain maximum information about the phenomena under the investigation with the least spending of money, time, and energy.

The present study made use of non probability sampling technique where in purposive sampling is considered most appropriate. In purposive sampling, the elements (or individuals) are selected by experts.

A common strategy of the purposive sampling is to pick cases that are judged to be typical of the population in which one is interested. Judgement sampling has great utility in exploring the details, which aim at obtaining insights that would go into all the details in terms of formulating hypotheses for the research (Kothari, 1985).

Details of the sample are presented in Tables 2, 3, and 4.

TABLE 2

Age-wise classification of subjects in the Experimental and Control Groups

Group	Age			Total
	30-39	40-49	50-59	
Experimental Group	10	39	11	60
Control group	9	35	16	60
Total	19	74	27	120

Table 2 indicates that majority of subjects in each group belong to the age group of 40-49 years.

TABLE 3

Sex-wise classification of subjects in the Experimental and Control groups

Group	Sex	
	Male	Female
Experimental group	54	6
Control group	51	9

From Table 3, it is evident that males are more in number when compare to females in both the experimental and the control groups.

TABLE 4

Religion-wise classification of subjects in the Experimental and Control Groups

Group	Religion			Total
	Hindu	Muslim	Christian	
Experimental Group	29	21	10	60
Control group	28	20	12	60
Total	57	41	22	120

Table 4 shows that Hindus are more in number when compared toChristians and Muslims, in both the experimental and controls groups.

While there are 57 Hindus, Muslims are 41, and Christians are 22, in a total of 120 subjects in the experimental and control groups.

Religion-wise classification of subjects thus indicates that Christians are less than half in number compared to Hindus.

B. TOOLS AND VARIABLES

The variables used for the present investigation were anxiety, depression, security feeling, stress tolerance, and quality of life. The psychological tests used for measuring the variables are detailed below.

(a) ANXIETY SCALE

Anxiety Scale (Abridged version) used for the present investigation was developed by Iby and Sananda Raj (2002 a).

Anxiety as used in the scale means states of worry, uneasiness, trembling, tension, fatigue, sleeping difficulties, and the like.

The term has been defined by Carson and Butcher (1992) as "generalized feelings of fear and apprehension".

The items for the scale had been adapted from Anxiety Scale Questionnaire developed by Krug with Scheler and Cattell (1976). There are both positive and negative items.

A total of 40 items were used for the draft scale. The procedure suggested by Anastasi (1971) followed for item analysis. Sixteen items having high discriminating power and average difficulty index were selected for the final scale.

Instructions:

Certain statements related to life experiences are given below. As far as you are concerned all these may not be true. Yet you are requested to give your responses for all the statements thinking that you may have to face such situations. You have to put a "✓" mark on any one of the three alternatives, Viz., 'a', 'b', and 'c' so as to indicate the extent of your agreement with the statement. Here 'a' denotes 'Yes', 'b' denotes 'Undecided' and 'c' denotes 'No'. Use 'b' only if you cannot possibly decide on 'a' or 'c'. Please do not omit any item.

Two sample items are given below as examples:

1. I seem to tremble when I have to face a difficult task ahead.
2. I feel restless as if I want something but not sure of what.

The subjects were required to mark their responses by putting a " ✓ "mark. After item analysis, 16 items were selected for the final scale. The reliability and validity of the scale are as follows.

Validity:

The validity has been established by the method of content validity and concurrent validity. Content validity is the adequacy with which a test measures representative components of the skill in question (Anastasi, 1971). Since the scale covers adequately various aspects or components of anxiety, the scale rightly claims content validity.

Further, the correlation coefficient obtained with General Anxiety Scale (Sananda Raj & Prasad, 1999), as external criterion, on a sample of 45 adults was found to be 0.74. As this coefficient is statistically significant and high the scale has concurrent validity.

Reliability:

The reliability of the Anxiety Scale was found using split-half method, on a sample of 50 adults. The half-test reliability was found to be 0.90. Using Spearman-Brown formula (Anastasi, 1971), the reliability of the whole scale was estimated and was found to be 0.95.

The above details indicate that the scale would yield valid and reliable scores of anxiety for the present study.

The instructions and items are prepared and presented in English as well as in the regional language, Malayalam.

A copy of the scale is given as Appendix A.

(b) DEPRESSION INVENTORY

Depression Inventory used for the present investigation was developed by Iby and Sananda Raj (2002 b). Here the term 'Depression' means emotional state characterized by extreme sadness, gloomy ruminations, feelings of worthlessness, loss of hope, and often apprehension (Carson and Butcher, 1992).

A total of 50 items has been used for the draft scale. The procedure suggested by Anastasi (1971) has been used for item analysis. Thirty items were selected for the final scale.

Instructions:

Certain statements related to life experiences are given below. As far as you are concerned all these may not be true. Yet you are requested to give your responses for all the statements thinking that you may have to face such situations. You have to put a " ✓ " mark on any one of the two alternatives, viz., 'Yes' and 'No', so as to indicate the extent of your agreement with the statement.

Two sample items are given below as examples:

1. I blame myself for all my shortcomings.
2. I feel sad very often.

The subjects are required to give their responses by putting a " ✓ "mark. The reliability and validity of the inventory are as follows:

Validity:

The concurrent validity of the inventory was estimated using Beck Depression Inventory (Beck, 1996), as external criterion. Both the inventories were administered on a sample of 45 adults, and the correlation between the scores obtained. The r thus obtained was 0.83, indicating that the inventory is valid.

Reliability:

Split-half reliability of the inventory was found by correlating the odd and even scores on a sample of 50 subjects. The reliability of the half test was found to be 0.84, and that of the whole test was estimated to be 0.91, using Spearman-Brown formula.

The details given above indicate that Depression Inventory is a reliable and valid instrument.

A copy of the Depression Inventory is given as Appendix B.

(c) SECURITY-INSECURITY FEELING INVENTORY

Security-Insecurity Feeling Inventory was developed by Iby and Sananda Raj (2002 c).

The term 'Security' as used in the present inventory means the feelings of being at home in the world, safety, friendliness, calm, easy, emotional stability, self-acceptance and well based self-feeling of strength.

Security can be defined as the conditions of being in safety, or free from threat of danger to life, or what is highly valued; employed in special sense by Adler, of a condition in which power or conquest is attained without struggle (Cited in Naqvi, 1986).

The inventory was to measure the feeling of security. Some of the items for the scale have been selected from other psychological tests, namely, Indian adaptation of Maslow's Security-Insecurity Feeling Inventory by Naqvi in the year 1986. The remaining items were developed by the investigator for the purpose of the present study. A total of 47 items has been used for the draft scale. The procedure suggested by the Anastasi (1971) has been used for item analysis. After item analysis, 30 items were selected for the final scale.

Instructions:

Certain statements related to life experiences are given below. As far as you are concerned all these may not be true. Yet you are requested to give your responses for all the statements, thinking that you may have to face such situations. You have to put a " ✓" mark on any one of the two alternatives, viz., 'Yes' and 'No' so as to indicate the extent of your agreement with the statement.

Two sample items are given below as examples:

1. Do you experience that life is a great burden?
2. Do you consider that the results of all activities are satisfying?

Scoring:

The subjects are required to mark their responses by putting a " ✓ " mark on any one of the two alternatives, viz., 'Yes' and 'No' so as to indicate the extent of the agreement with the statement. The scale contains equal number of positive and negative items. For the positive statements, a weightage of 2 is given for 'Yes' responses and a weightage of 1 for 'No' responses. The procedure is reversed for negative statements.

Validity:

The validity of the scale has been established by correlating the scores obtained by the test by another test namely, The Inferiority and Insecurity Questionnaires (Pati, 1976). The correlation coefficient was estimated as 0.72 (N=45), indicating that the inventory has concurrent validity.

Reliability:

The odd-even reliability of the inventory, estimated on a sample of 50 adults, was found to be 0.96 (the half-test reliability being 0.92).

The above coefficients are significant at 0.01 level, and indicate that the inventory is valid and reliable.

A copy of Security-Insecurity Feeling Inventory is given on Appendix C.

(d) STRESS TOLERANCE SCALE

The term stress is taken here to mean psychological stress. Psychological stress involves demands on the organism which are perceived to be beyond its coping capacity. It includes the cognitive demands in terms of upsetting the steady flow of life, as well as the systemic stress in terms of known physiological response within the organism. If coping is successful, the organism comes back to the normal state. Psychological disturbances associated with stress, not effectively coped may upset the body chemistry. Factors which help a person to tolerate stress, or are associated with increased stress tolerance- intra-individual and extra-individual-may help in building resistance.

Selye (1976) regards stress as a non-specific response of the body to the demands made upon it. The cycle which the organism goes through under stress is termed the general adaptation syndrome, consisting of the stages of a. alarm reaction, b. resistance, and c. exhaustion.

For measuring stress tolerance, the psychological test namely Stress Tolerance Scale constructed and standardized by Reshmy and Sananda Raj (1999) has been used The scale consisted of 24 items.

Instructions:

Certain statements related to life experiences are given below. As far as you are concerned all these may not be true. Yet you are requested to give your response for all the statements thinking that you may have to face such situations. You have to put a (✓) mark on any of the five alternatives, viz., A, B, C, D or E so as to indicate the extent of your agreement with the statement. A stands for

Strongly agree, B Agree, C Undecided, D Disagree and E Strongly disagree. Please do not omit any item. Your response will be kept confidential and will be used for research purpose only.

Two examples of the items are given below:

1. I am unable to tolerate the criticisms of others.
2. I can withstand any situation rising out of unstable income.

The subjects are required to mark their responses by putting a "✓" mark on any of the five alternatives, viz., A, B, C, D or E so as to indicate the extent of agreement with the statement. A stands for Strongly Agree, B- Agree, C - Undecided D-Disagree and E-Strongly Disagree.

The scale contains both positive and negative items, the positive statements carrying a weightage of 5, 4, 3, 2, and 1 for answers A, B, C, D, and E respectively and it is reversed for negative items. The scores of the 24 items were added to get a final score. The details of validity and reliability provided in the manual of the scale (Reshmi & Sananda Raj, 1999) are given below:

Validity:

The validity of the test was estimated with the help of empirical/criterion related validity. It was found out by correlating the "Stress Tolerance Scale" with "Stress Tolerance Inventory" developed by Balagangadharan (1988). The correlation coefficient was estimated as 0.87. This index of validity shows that Stress Tolerance Scale is adequately valid. This value is significant at 0.01 level.

Reliability:

Split-half reliability method was used to estimate the reliability of the test. The test was split into two equal halves on the basis of odd items and even items (odd even reliability method). A correlation coefficient between the two halves was found using Carl Pearson's Product Moment Formula. Thus the half test reliability coefficient of 0.80 was obtained. The reliability of the whole test was estimated using Spearman-Brown formula. The reliability coefficient thus obtained was 0.89. This index of reliability shows that Stress Tolerance Scale is highly reliable. This value of reliability is significant at 0.01 level.

A copy of Stress Tolerance Scale is given as Appendix D.

(E) QUALITY OF LIFE SCALE

The term Quality of Life (QOL) as used in the scale indicates 'the subjective perceived satisfaction in one's different aspects of life as reported by the individual (Szalai & Andrews, 1980).

QOL emphasizes one's immediate, self-experienced well-being, satisfaction in life, happiness, and fulfillment of needs (Ventegodt, Holden, & Zachau Christiansen, 1991).

For measuring quality of life, the psychological test namely, Quality of Life Scale, constructed and standardized by Warrier and Sananda Raj (1999) has been used. This test has 3 subtests measuring physical aspects (Section A), psychological aspects (Section B), and the social aspects (Section C) of quality of life. It is a five-point scale, consisting of 30 items.

Instructions:

Some statements relating to certain aspects of your life are given below. Read each statement carefully and indicate how much you agree with each statement. Your response can be strongly agree, agree, undecided, disagree or strongly disagree. Indicate your choice by placing a "✓" mark on any of the five alternatives, viz., A, B, C, D or E so as to indicate the extent of your agreement with the statement. A stands for Strongly agree, B - agree, C - Undecided, D - disagree, and E-Strongly disagree.

The response Undecided should be selected when you can't say clearly either you agree or disagree with the situation.

Please do not omit items. Your responses will be used strictly for research purpose and will be kept confidential.

Two examples of the items are given below:

1. I feel that I am generally healthy.
2. I am not satisfied with my sleep patterns.

The scoring of this test is same as that of the Stress Tolerance Scale by Reshmi and Sananda Raj. Here the maximum possible score of the scale is 150, and the minimum 30.

The validity and reliability as given in the manual are as follows:

Validity:

Concurrent validity of Quality of Life Scale is estimated using Quality of Life Index (by Ferrans & Powers, 1985), as external criterion, and the correlation coefficient obtained was found to be 0.81, which indicates that the test has high validity.

Reliability:

Split-half method is used to find the reliability. It was found to be 0.81 for the half-test and 0.90, for the whole test, after correction for attenuation.

These details indicate that the scale would yield valid and reliable measure of quality of life of the subjects under study.

A copy of Quality of Life Scale is given as Appendix E.

Psychometric Properties of the Tests used for the Study: A Brief Overview:

A brief overview of the relevant details of the psychological tests used for the present investigation is presented in Table 5.

TABLE 5

Summary of reliability and validity, and other relevant information about Tests used for the present study

Author(s)	Year	Name of Test/ Scale	Reliability *		Validity *	
			Half test	Whole test	External criterion	Coefficient
Iby and Sananda Raj	2002 a	Anxiety Scale (Abridged Version)	.90	.95	General Anxiety Scale (Sananda Raj & Prasad, 1999)	.74
Iby and Sananda Raj	2002 b	Depression Inventory	.84	.91	Beck Depression Inventory (Beck, 1996)	.83
Iby and Sananda Raj	2002 c	Security-Insecurity Feeling Inventory	.92	.96	The Inferiority and Insecurity Questionnaire (Pati, 1976)	.72
Reshmi and Sananda Raj	1999	Stress Tolerance Scale	.80	.89	Stress Tolerance Inventory (Balagangadharan, 1988)	.87
Warrier and Sananda Raj	1999	Quality of Life Scale	.81	.90	Quality of Life Index (Ferrans & Powers, 1985)	.81

Note: *All the coefficients of reliability and validity are significant at 0.01 level.

C. DATA COLLECTION PROCEDURE

The data collection procedure for the present investigation may be briefly brought under two heads:

(i) Data collection for quantitative analysis

(ii) Data collection for qualitative analysis

Standardized psychological tests and personal information schedule (described earlier) were used to collect data from the subjects. The data thus collected formed the basis of quantitative analysis. For qualitative study, interview, observation, and relevant documents were the major sources of data. The details of the procedure for analysis are given below:

D. STATISTICAL TECHNIQUES USED FOR QUANTITATIVE ANALYSIS

The study employed certain statistical tools to test the hypotheses. A theoretical note on the techniques and the rationale for their use appear in the following section.

1. The t-test (to compare the experimental and control group) for anxiety, depression, security feeling, stress tolerance, and quality of life.

2. The Pearson r (to find out the correlations among the variables under study).

1. The t-test

The t-test or test of significance of the difference between means for large independent samples (Garrett, 1969) is used to compare the means of the two groups on each of the variables.

The ratio of deviation of scores from the mean or other parameter in a distribution of sample statistics, to the standard error of that distribution is designated as 't' (Guilford, 1965). Usually the t-test is used for comparison of the difference between means of two groups.

1. Single group method

In single group design, the significance of the difference between correlated means obtained from the same test administered to the same group upon two occasions is used. This experimental design is called the single group method. Here, in the present investigation, a group of five tests were administered to the CHD patients initially; later, the same tests were repeated in order to measure the effect of the investigation programme (viz., relaxation, meditation, and visualization). In other words, this method is used to estimate the effect of the interpolated activity (relaxation, meditation, and visualization) between test and retest.

2. Two group method

Here in the present investigation, the experimental groups namely, the intervention group and the control group (non intervention group) were used to compare the difference between them for the five variables under study.

Also, the initial test data (pre-test data) for the experimental and the control groups were compared using t-test.

2. Correlation

Problems which involve the relationship of one variable to another can be studied by the method of correlation. If two variables correlate with each other, there is reason to believe in the existence of a common relationship. It may be noted, however, that cause-effect relationships cannot be inferred from this information alone; additional criteria would be required (Child, 1990). The standard kind of coefficient of correlation and the one most commonly computed is the Pearson's Product Moment Coefficient (Pearson r).

Statistical Procedure Used in Interpreting r :

1. Verbal Interpretation of Correlation:

The product moment coefficient of correlation between any two variables can be described in a general way as high, marked or substantial and low or negligible.

Garrett (1969) presents the following classification for interpreting the various values of r's:

r from .00 to ± .20 denotes indifferent or negligible relationship;
r from ± .20 to ± .40 denotes low correlation present but slight;
r from ± .40 to ± .70 denotes substantial or marked relationship; and
r from ± .70 to ± 1.00 denotes high to very high relationship.

2. *The significance of r:*

The significance of an obtained r may be tested against the hypothesis that the population r is in fact zero. If the computed r is large enough to invalidate these null hypotheses, we accept r as indicating the presence of at least some degree of correlation.

To make the test, we refer to the table-values, with N-2 degrees of freedom, and compare the obtained r with the tabulated entries. Two significance levels, 0.05 and 0.01, are given in the table.

In the present investigation, the table values corresponding to 0.05 level is 0.180 and that corresponding to 0.01 level is 0.235, since N=120 (df = 120–2=118). This means that we consider those r's which are greater than 0.235 are significant at 0.01 level and those above 0.180 and below 0.235 as significant at 0.05 level.

Only if the obtained r is significant, it is verbally interpreted.

3. *Percentage Overlap of Correlated Variables:*

The Pearson r between two variables can be interpreted in terms of common variance for the two variables (overlap). The percentage overlap equals $r^2 \times 100$ (Garrett, 1969).

E. PROCEDURE FOR QUALITATIVE ANALYSIS

All qualitative research methods have in common the use of qualitative data (Best & Kahn, 1995). A variety of terms have been used for the various forms of qualitative methods. Case study is one of them.

Qualitative research uses different forms of data compared to those used in traditional research methods. Qualitative methods consist of three kinds of data collection: In-depth open-ended interviews, direct observation, and written documents. The data from interviews consist of direct quotation from people about their experiences, opinions, feelings, knowledge. The data from observation consists of detailed description of people's activities, actions, and the range of interpersonal interactions, and organizational processes that are part of observable human experiences.

Since case study was used in the present investigation and interview and observation techniques were employed for the purpose of collecting, a brief narration of these methods is presented below.

I. Case study

Case study implies 'assessment information on a specific individual' (Carson & Butcher, 1992). Case studies have been done elaborately so that a detailed description of the cases can be qualitatively analyzed. Data for the purpose of the present investigation have been collected using the techniques of interview and observation as the major tools. Details were also collected from the relevant psychological tests, from the documents maintained in the hospital, and also from the spouses of the patients.

2. Interview

The term interview stands for a general concept which includes a variety of procedures adapted in collecting data through person to person contact between an interviewer and a respondent. The basic objective of the interview is to secure information from the person who alone knows the subjects or matter, which is required by the interviewer.

The interviewer must approach an interview at a time when the person is free and in a relaxed mood. Before starting the interview, the interviewer must give his full introduction to the respondent. For accurate information, the members of the family should also be interviewed.

The most obvious way to measure attitudes and behaviour is to ask subjects how they feel, what they are thinking, or what they do or have done. By interviewing subjects, and having them answer questionnaires, a great deal of important information can be obtained. The most common ways of collecting self-report data are by administering questionnaires and by interviewing people.

In clinical interview, the basic purpose is to ascertain the causes and other relevant information related to the basic question. In focused interview, the main purpose is to get information related to the basic themes.

The key to interviewing is the extent to which the interviewer can establish rapport. It is a somewhat intangible quality that may be both a personal quality and developed ability.

All these points are taken care of in conducting interviews with the coronary heart disease patients, as part of case study.

3. Observation

Observation method is a systematic technique conducted by observers who are trained to watch and record behaviour without bias. In observational method, the researcher watches others and report their behaviour and interactions in a given setting. The advantage of observational method over other techniques is the opportunity to gain first-hand knowledge of the way people behave. In the present investigation, observation method is also made use of as a technique for obtaining relevant data from the CHD patients.

F. TECHNIQUES OF LIFE STYLE MODIFICATION PROGRAMME

(a) ABDOMINAL BREATHING

Abdominal breathing or diaphragmatic breathing is one of the simplest yet most powerful stress management techniques. Breathing from the abdomen lowers your center of gravity and thus increases your stability during sparring.

Introductory statement to be announced for the information of the patient:

Diaphragmatic breathing increases the suction pressure in your chest, thereby improving venous return of blood to your heart.

When the diaphragm contracts, this large muscle is forced downwards, causing a partial vacuum that forces air into the lungs (Ornish, 1996).

***Instructions*:**

To practice abdominal breathing, sit comfortably with the back straight. If at all possible, always breathe through the nose, which filters and warms the air. Place your right hand on your chest and your left hand on your abdomen. This will help you to be aware of your abdominal muscles as you breathe.

Concentrate on contracting your diaphragm and breathing from deep down within your abdomen. As you begin to inhale, your left hand should begin to rise, but your right hand should move very little.

Now exhale as much air as you can, while contracting your abdominal muscles. Once again, your left hand should move in as you exhale but your right hand should move very little. This is abdominal breathing. While it may feel unnatural at first, breathing from your abdomen will gradually become automatic if you practice it on a regular basis.

After a while, you will breathe from your abdomen most of the time, even when you are asleep. When you are able to do this, then you will feel less stressed and more balanced.

(b) PROGRESSIVE DEEP RELAXATION

The ability to respond to stress and the ability to relax are equally important in being able to function effectively while remaining healthy. The ideal response is to respond to challenges or difficult situations fast and efficiently and then to relax.

***Initial requirements*:**

Proper lighting and ventilation should be there in the room for relaxation. The room should be very comfortable with adequate space and with fewer disturbances. The skilled psychologist in this area should administer the relaxation technique. She should avail the necessary facilities like cot with out bed and pillow, chairs etc. The trainer should maintain a good rapport with the coronary heart disease patients.

Instructions to the client

Steps:

1. Lie on your back with your eyes closed. Move around a little until you feel comfortable, and then try to lie without moving. Begin by inhaling, tensing your right leg and raising it a few inches off the ground.....hold it there for a few seconds...and then let it drop to the floor as you exhale. Repeat the same with the left leg.

(Pause whenever required)

2. Inhale deeply and contract the muscles of your right arm as you raise it a few inches off the ground, hold it there for about five seconds; and let it drop to the floor as you exhale.

    Do the same with the left arm.

(Pause whenever required)

3. Now inhale deeply and contract the muscles of your buttocks as you raise your pelvis a few inches off the ground; hold it there for about five seconds; and let it drop to the floor as you exhale.

(Pause whenever required)

4. Inhale deeply and push your abdomen out like a balloon; hold your breath for about five seconds while contracting your abdomen; and let your abdomen completely relax as you exhale.

    Repeat the same sequence with your upper chest.

(Pause whenever required)

5. Leaving your arms relaxed, inhale, bring your shoulders up toward your ears; bring them together in front of your chest; and push them toward your feet.

    Relax.

(Pause whenever required)

6. Inhale deeply and stretch your neck backwards and allow your neck to relax completely as you exhale.

   Relax.

(Pause whenever required)

7. Inhale deeply and squeeze together all of your facial muscles, including your jaw, mouth, eyes, and forehead. Then relax. Finally, mentally allow each part of your body to relax even more.

(Pause whenever required)

8. Bring your awareness to your breathing. Without trying to change your pattern of breathing, just observe or feel the gentle flow of air as it comes in and out of your nose. After a few minutes, or whenever you wish, gradually allow your inhalations to become a little deeper with each breath. Imagine that you are breathing in light and healing energy as well as oxygen that is revitalizing and recharging your body and mind. Slowly move your fingers and toes, hands and feet.

Then gently roll your arms and legs back and forth. When you are ready, slowly roll over onto your side, and then come to a seated position.

(Pause whenever required)

The Progressive deep relaxation will last about 15-20 minutes. Towards the end of the programme, a feeling of relaxation will experience by the patients. We can see the relaxation from the face itself against the tensed facial muscles.

(c) VISUALIZATION

Visualization is creating a picture in your mind. It is easy to do after meditating because meditation helps to focus one's awareness. Visualization is not wishful thinking or fantasy, both of which are unfocused and passive. It is direct and active; it is a therapeutic use of meditation.

During meditation the patients of coronary heart disease can visualize the clearing up of blockages in their coronary arteries and the resumption of blood supply to the heart muscles.

Visualization is an imaginative process of forming pictures in the mind's eye. When we visualize in a non-meditative mood, i.e., when our mind is full of other thoughts, visualization is not effective because it is unfocussed and passive.

However, during meditation, visualization becomes active and focused. Like the sunrays converging through a magnifying glass burn the paper, visualization during meditation brings about the desired effects. In our program the participants visualize in a variety of ways: how their coronary circulation and function of heart improve and how they feel energetic in their daily routine. The beauty of this visualization is that though there may be no anatomical or physiological relevance to their imagination, even then it improves the clinical condition of the patient.

Dr. Dean Ornish has noted it to be useful to his participants. Visualization also includes forgiving an individual who has done a great wrong or injustice to you in the past. Visualization is most challenging and perhaps the most powerful of all the techniques in this programme of coronary healing. At one time or the other, all of us are apt to be treated unfairly. We often respond by getting angry. When this anger is not resolved in a constructive way, we may internalise it and carry it with you from day to day. Anger is not always inappropriate.

Sometimes it is quiet healthy to be angry, if you express it constructively and let it go. It is when you hold on to anger, long after it has served its purpose, that it may become destructive. After a while this emotional stress may produce chronic injuries to the walls of arteries. Such a stress can be resolved by forgiving the person during visualization.

How to Perform Directed Visualization

Visualization can be done using any and all of your senses. Even if you don't "see" mental images in your mind's eye, you might "hear" sounds, "taste" food, "smell" fragrances, or "touch" something or someone. For example, some people visualize detailed scenes in color, whereas others imagine only the rough outlines of a scene in black and white. There is no right or wrong way to visualize, only what works for you.

The Healing Heart Visualization - Instructions:

If you have heart disease, ask your cardiologist for a diagram showing the exact location of each of your coronary artery blockages. This can be helpful in the visualization process. A diagram for visualization is given as Figure 2.

Fig . 2 . Diagram for visualization

Now choose a healing image that incorporates the following:

- Your heart is beating regularly.
- Your heart is pumping a healthy amount of blood with each beat.
- The arteries in your heart are dilating and allowing more blood to flow.
- New blood vessels are growing and supplying oxygen and other nutrients to your heart.
- The blood is flowing smoothly and unobstructed.

If you don't have a known heart problem, then just choose an image in which your heart is healthy. As with any visualization, adding detail may be useful. You may want to check out some medical books showing various pictures of hearts. Or you may even want to watch a film of a heart during surgery.

You can visualize your heart improving at any time, but it is most effective when done following meditation, because meditation helps to focus your awareness.

5. MEDITATION

Meditation has begun to occupy a significant place in the conventional treatment of coronary heart disease. It has come to stay as an essential part of management along with medication and surgery. Meditation is the process of quieting our mind. When the mind is quiet, we will feel peaceful. The practice of meditation can be very challenging, for it is not very easy to quiet one's own mind.

Meditation is simply being in the present moment. The present moment frees the individual to change, explore new patterns, pleasures, and possibilities. Meditation allows to go deeper, to where the disturbances begin. It helps to become more aware of how the mind becomes agitated and gives the individual more control to stop these disturbances.

Most of the time, we are not fully aware of what we are doing or experiencing.

The first step of every approach to meditation is paying attention. Paying attention, or increasing awareness, is the beginning of healing. Meditation keeps us in present tense; anxiety, fear, worry, and depression are concerns about past and future events. When we are in the present moment, even difficult situations need not cause us to feel intensely stressed.

Meditation, as a process of learning to train the mind, helps one do what one wants more effectively. When one is learned to meditate, he was able to focus better on the task at hand rather than worrying about the future.

When we worry about the future, then we lose twice : We may miss the joy of the present moment, and decrease the chances of future success. The present moment is joyful. The present moment is sensual – Paying attention enhances all sensual experiences. When we meditate regularly, our ability to keep our attention focused begins to increase.

How to Meditate

There are many types of meditation. Here are some of the most simple yet powerful:

- Focusing on your breathing
- Focusing on a sound (religious or secular)
- Mindfulness
- Self-analysis
- Prayer or devotion

We can meditate anywhere, at any time. Many people find it beneficial, to meditate twice daily for at least five to thirty minutes, once in the morning and once in the evening. Twenty minutes twice a day seems about right for many people. Some teachers advise that dawn and dusk are the ideal times for meditation. It's better to meditate for only a few minutes on a regular basis than to do it for longer on an irregular basis.

(1) *FOCUS ON YOUR BREATHING*

INSTRUCTIONS:

There are many ways to meditate. No one way is best for everyone. One thing common to all forms of meditation is the art of paying attention. We do a lot of different things at the same time.

In order to mediate, ***first pay attention to breathing***. Breathing is central to every aspect of meditation training. It is a wonderful place to ***focus the mind.***

Breath is a rich experience. It connects us with the whole universe. When you try to pay attention to breathing, you notice that the mind starts wandering. The wandering of the mind is a normal state of mind. From the meditative perspective the normal state of mind is severely sub-optimal. It is more asleep than awake.

Set aside a special room or at least an area within a room used only for meditation. After a while, we will associate that area with meditation, and we will begin to feel more peaceful just being there. With practice, we can bring that state of enhanced awareness to everything you do.

Begin by assuming a comfortable position in a quiet place and closing your eyes. Sit still. Without changing how you breathe, simply observe the air coming in and going out. Notice how the air feels as it comes in and goes out. Then observe the pauses between each inhalation and exhalation. When you exhale, count "one".

The next time you exhale, count "two" and so on. After your fifth exhalation, start over again and count "one", "two", back up to five. Only count when you exhale. (If you find yourself counting higher than five, then you know your mind is wandering.) Mentally count your breaths. Another approach is to allow your body to relax each time you exhale. The goal is not to stop all thoughts; it is to focus on only one thing, your breathing.

(2) FOCUS ON SOUND

Sounds are powerful. Different sounds can alter our state of mind in powerful ways. Some sounds, like military music on the battlefield make us agitated or aggressive. Other sounds, like a waterfall or lullaby, are relaxing. These sounds influence us even when there is no work or literal meaning associated with them.

A time-honoured way of focusing the mind is to meditate by repeating a sound over and over. The sound can be secular (for example, repeating the word "one") or religious. Choose a sound that is comfortable and is consistent with your own belief system.

The most basic sound is humming. During times of deep meditation, when your body is relaxed and your mind is very quiet and still, you can hear a low-pitched, continuous humming sound.

According to meditative tradition, all sounds are derived from this one. This humming sound is very peaceful. Sometimes these sounds are literally translated to mean "peace", such as "*om*" in Sanskrit, "*shalom*" in Hebrew, "*salam*" in Arabic, "ameen" in the Muslim tradition, and so on.

When you meditate, you may want to choose a word that incorporates one of these sounds. In any event, use a word, sound, or phrase that it is consistent with your own beliefs and values.

According to meditation teachers, repeating one of these sounds over and over has a double benefit. First, it focuses your awareness. Also, the sound creates a peaceful state, like tuning a radio.

When you meditate, sit in a comfortable position in a quiet place and close your eyes, ***Inhale***, then repeat the word, sound, or phrase as you Exhale. There is no "right" way to do this; find a tempo and tone that leave you feeling calm and comfortable. When your mind wanders, gently bring it back to repeating the word or phrase. Since it is perfectly normal for your mind to wander, don't get upset when this happens. When you notice that you are thinking about something other than the sound, just bring it back to the sound over and over again.

After you have spent a while repeating this sound or phrase out loud, then begin repeating it silently. The effect is more subtle, yet in many ways even more powerful when you repeat a sound or phrase silently, although your mind may tend to wander more than when saying it out loud. Also, you can meditate silently anywhere: on the bus, on the train, while waiting in line, and so on.

Human beings have a capacity of shifting their awareness wherever they wish. Normally, individuals who have not been trained to meditate keep their awareness on the mind which has the habit of wandering. Cultivating and developing a capacity to keep ***the awareness in the present moment instead of the wandering mind*** is all that what meditation is about.

When you start focusing your awareness on breathing, you begin to ride the waves of breath, in and out. At this moment, the awareness begins to wander to the thoughts. Willingly, gently and kindly bring it back to the breath. If it wanders a million times, just lasso it back to breath a million times. This will train the mind to settle at one place.

Meditation is a way of living which introduces us to that other part of our consciousness which is the common ground of all humanity. In meditation we experience the emptiness of the concept of separate existence. This frees us from the qualities that separate us, and it generates in us compassion, love, and altruism which unite us.

(3) MINDFULNESS

Mindfulness is the process of paying attention to everything that you do. In that sense, the life becomes a continual meditation, not simply the fifteen or twenty minutes that you spend observing the breathing or repeating a sound. The essence of mindfulness is to pay attention without judging and without preconceptions.

Keeping your eyes closed, bring the awareness to the thoughts. Without trying to control or direct them, just observe each thought as it comes into the mind - as if you were watching a movie entitled, "Thoughts", observing without preconceptions or judgments.

(4) SELF-ANALYSIS

Self-analysis can also allow us to discriminate what is real from what is not.

(5) PRAYER OR DEVOTION

Mind, body and spirit are all intimately interconnected. Because of this, coronary heart disease occurs on emotional and spiritual levels as well as physical ones. If we limit our treatments only to the physical heart, then the disease tends to come back again and again-or the treatments may be worse than the illness.

CHAPTER IV

ANALYSIS AND DISCUSSION

A. Single-group design: Analysis and interpretation
B. Two-group design: Analysis and interpretation
C. Correlation analysis
D. Case study: The presentation and comments
E. Treadmill test

A. SINGLE GROUP DESIGN: ANALYSIS AND INTREPRETATION

The t-Test :

The t-test was done in order to find out whether there existed any significant difference between the scores obtained by the experimental group of coronary heart disease patients (intervention group) before and after intervention, for the different variables used in the present investigation.

The details are given below:

(a) Comparison of Anxiety Scores of Coronary Heart Disease Patients (Intervention Group) Before and After Intervention:

For the variable Anxiety, the mean value obtained by the intervention group of CHD patients before intervention was 29.5 and after intervention was 24.78. The standard errors were 0.426 and 0.350 respectively.

The correlation between the scores of anxiety obtained by the subjects before and after intervention was 0.42. The t-value obtained was 12.22.

The details of the t-test are given in Table 6.

TABLE 6

Before and After Scorse of Intervention Group:
Data and Results of t-test for Anxiety

Anxiety	Mean	SE	r	t-Value
Before Intervention	29.95	0.426	0.42	12.22 *
After Intervention	24.78	0.350		

Note: * indicates significance at 0.01 level.

The results indicated that there was significant difference between the scores for the variable Anxiety, for the CHD patients of the intervention group before and after intervention. This means that the level of anxiety got reduced after intervention, showing the effect of relaxation, meditation, and visualization on CHD patients.

It may be mentioned here that the previous study conducted by Buselli and Stuart (1999) is supported by the present investigation. These investigators had shown that anxiety would be reduced on the patients because of the intervention strategies.

However, the present study did not support the findings of Jones and West (1996) and Janne (2000), which did not find any significant change in anxiety due to intervention.

(b) Comparison of Depression Scores of CHD Patients (Intervention Group) Before and After Intervention:

For the Depression, the mean value obtained by the intervention group of CHD patients before intervention was 38.36 and after intervention was 34.71. The standard errors were 0.631 and 0.551respectively.

The correlation between the scores of depression obtained by the subjects before and after intervention was 0.61. The t-value obtained was 6.93. The details of the t-test are given in Table 7.

TABLE 7

Before and After Scorse of Intervention Group:
Data and Results of t-test for Depression

Depression	Mean	SE	r	t-Value
Before Intervention	38.36	0.631	0.61	6.93*
After Intervention	34.71	0.551		

Note: * indicates significance at 0.01 level.

The results indicated that there was significant difference between the scores for the variable Depression, for the CHD patients of the intervention group before and after intervention. This means that the level of Depression got reduced after intervention, showing the effect of relaxation, meditation, and visualization on CHD patients.

The results of the studies conducted by Busselli and Stuart (1999), and Carney (2000) were supported by the present investigation, in the sense that there studies indicated significant reduction in depression due to intervention.

The present study did not support the findings of Jones and West (1996), Irvine (1999), Jane (2000) and Lane (2001), which showed that intervention strategies had no significant effect.

(c) *Comparison of Security Feeling Scores of CHD Patients (Intervention Group) Before and After Intervention:*

For the variable Security Feeling, the mean value obtained by the intervention group of coronary heart disease patients before intervention was 51.92 and after intervention was 56.13. The standard errors were 0.575 and 0.422 respectively.

The correlation between the scores of security feeling obtained by the subjects before and after intervention was 0.59. The t-value obtained was –8.92.

The details of the t-test are given in Table 8.

TABLE 8

Before and After Scorse of Intervention Group:
Data and Results of t-test for Security Feeling

Security Feeling	Mean	SE	r	t-Value
Before Intervention	51.92	0.575	0.59	-8.92*
After Intervention	56.13	0.422		

Note: * indicates significance at 0.01 level.

The results indicated that there was significant difference between the scores for the variable Security Feeling, for the CHD patients of the intervention group before and after intervention. This means that the level of Security Feeling got increased after intervention, showing the effect of relaxation, meditation, and visualization on CHD patients.

(d) Comparison of Stress Tolerance Scores of Intervention Group Before and After intervention:

For the variable Stress Tolerance, the mean value for before intervention was 51.92 and after intervention was 56.13. The standard errors are 1.67 and 1.53 respectively. The correlation between the scores of stress tolerance obtained by the subjects before and after intervention was 0.47. The t-value obtained was -9.99.

The details of the t-test are given in Table 9.

TABLE 9

Before and After Scorse of Intervention Group:
Data and Results of t-test for Stress Tolerance

Stress Tolerance	Mean	SE	r	t-Value
Before Intervention	61.14	1.67	0.47	-9.99*
After Intervention	77.65	1.53		

Note: * indicates significance at 0.01 level.

The results indicated that there was significant difference between the scores for the variable Stress Tolerance, for the CHD patients of the intervention group before and after intervention. This means that the level of stress tolerance got increased after intervention, showing the effect of relaxation, meditation, and visualization on CHD patients.

(e) Comparison of Quality of Life scores of Intervention Group Before and After intervention:

For the variable Quality of life, the mean value for before intervention was 102.25 and after intervention was 114.67. The standard errors are 1.31 and 2.13 respectively. The correlation between the scores of stress tolerance obtained by the subjects before and after intervention was 0.78. The t-value obtained was -9.01.

The details of the t-test are given in Table 10.

TABLE 10

Before and After Scorse of Intervention Group:
Data and Results of t-test for Quality of Life

Quality of Life	Mean	SE	r	t-Value
Before Intervention	102.25	1.31	0.78	-9.01*
After Intervention	114.67	2.13		

Note: * indicates significance at 0.01 level.

The results indicated that there was significant difference between the scores for the variable Quality of Life, for the CHD patients of the intervention group before and after intervention. This means that the level of Quality of Life got increased after intervention, showing the effect of relaxation, meditation, and visualization on CHD patients.

The studies conducted by Arendarczyk and Loboz-Grudzien (2000) and Ornish (1990) are supported by the present investigation, since these had shown that Quality of Life of coronary heart disease patients increased due to the intervention strategies.

B. TWO-GROUP DESIGN : ANALYSIS AND INTERPRETATION

The t-test : Comparison of Pre-Test Data of Control and Experimental Groups

(a) Comparison of Anxiety Scores of Control and Experimental Groups of CHD patients Before Intervention:

The experimental and control groups of coronary heart disease patients were compared for the variable Anxiety. The mean values of anxiety before intervention were 28.81 and after intervention were 29.92. The standard deviations were 4.16 and 3.30 respectively. The t-value obtained was -1.65.

The details of the t-test are given in Table 11 .

TABLE 11

Before intervention scores of experimental and control groups:
Results of t-test for anxiety

Anxiety	Mean	SD	t-Value	Level of Significance
Experimental Group	28.81	4.16	-1.65	N S
Control Group	29.95	3.30		

Note: The t-value is not significant statistically.

The results indicated that there was no significant difference between the mean scores for the variable Anxiety obtained by the CHD patients of the experimental and the control groups before intervention. This indicates that the levels of Anxiety of both the experimental as well as the control group were the same, initially.

(b) Comparison of Depression Scores of Experimental and Control Groups of CHD Patients Before Intervention:

The experimental and control groups of coronary heart disease patients were compared for the variable Depression. The mean values of depression before intervention was 37.42 and after intervention was 38.37. The standard deviations were 6.31 and 4.89 respectively. The t-value obtained was -0.91. The details of the t-test are given in Table 12.

TABLE 12

Before intervention scores of experimental and control groups:
Results of t-test for depression

Depression	Mean	SD	t-Value	Level of Significance
Experimental Group	37.42	6.31	-0.91	N S
Control Group	38.37	4.89		

Note: The t-value is not significant statistically.

The results indicated that there was no significant difference between the mean scores for the variable Depression obtained by the CHD patients of both the experimental and control groups before intervention.

This means that the levels of depression of both the experimental as well as the control groups were the same, initially.

(c) Comparison of Security Feeling Scores of Experimental and Control Groups of CHD Patients Before intervention:

The experimental and control groups of coronary heart disease patients were compared for the variable Security Feeling, before intervention, as in the case of the other variables discussed above.

The mean values of Security Feeling obtained by experimental and control groups before intervention was 53.10 and 51.92 respectively. The corresponding standard deviations were 5.67 and 4.46. The t-value obtained was 1.27.

The details of the t-test are given in Table 13.

TABLE 13

Before intervention scores of experimental and control groups:
Results of t-test for security feeling

Security Feeling	Mean	SD	t-Value	Level of Significance
Experimental Group	53.10	5.67	1.27	N S
Control Group	51.92	4.46		

Note: The t-value is not significant statistically.

The results indicated that there was no significant difference between the mean scores for the variable Security Feeling obtained by the CHD patients of the experimental and the control groups before intervention. This indicates that the levels of Security Feeling of both the experimental as well as the control group were the same, initially.

(d) Comparison of Stress Tolerance Scores of Experimental and Control Groups of CHD Patients Before Intervention Period:

The experimental and control groups of coronary heart disease patients were compared for the Stress Tolerance. The mean values of stress tolerance before intervention was 60.36 and after intervention was 61.14. The standard deviations were 11.94 and 12.91 respectively. The t-value obtained was -0.34.

The details of the t-test are given in Table 14.

TABLE 14

Before intervention scores of experimental and control groups:
Results of t-test for stress tolerance

Stress Tolerance	Mean	SD	t-Value	Level of Significance
Experimental Group	60.36	11.94	-0.34	N S
Control Group	61.14	12.91		

Note: The t-value is not significant statistically.

The results indicated that there was no significant difference between the mean scores for the variable Stress Tolerance obtained by the CHD patients of the experimental and the control groups before intervention. This indicates that the levels of Security Feeling of both the experimental as well as the control group were the same, initially.

(e) Comparison of Quality of Life Scores of Experimental and Control Groups of CHD Patients Before Intervention:

The experimental and control groups of coronary heart disease patients were compared for the variable Quality of Life. The mean values of quality of life before intervention were 104.02 and after intervention were 102.25. The standard deviations were 12.89 and 10.13 respectively. The t-value obtained was 0.83.

The details of the t-test are given in Table 15.

TABLE 15

Before intervention scores of experimental and control groups:
Results of t-test for quality of life

Quality of Life	Mean	SD	t-Value	Level of Significance
Control Group	104.02	12.89	0.83	N S
Experimental Group	102.25	10.13		

Note: *The t-value is not significant statistically.*

The results indicated that there was no significant difference between the mean scores for the variable Quality of Life obtained by the CHD patients of the experimental and the control groups before intervention. This indicates that the levels of Quality of Life of both the experimental as well as the control group were the same, initially.

2. *The t-test : Comparison of post-test data of Experimental and Control Groups*

(a) *Comparison of Anxiety Scores of Experimental and Control Groups of CHD Patients After Intervention:*

For the variable Anxiety, the mean value for the experimental group was 24.78 after intervention, and for the control group after the intervention period were 26.40. The standard deviations were 2.77and 3.02 respectively. The t-value obtained was -4.95.

The details of the t-test are given in Table 16.

TABLE 16

After intervention scores of experimental and control groups: Results of t-test for anxiety

Anxiety	Mean	SD	t-value	Level of Significance
Experimental Group	24.78	2.77	-4.95	0.01
Control Group	26.40	3.02		

Note: The t-value is significant statistically.

The results indicated that there was significant difference between the scores for the variable Anxiety, for the experimental and control groups after intervention. This means that the level of Anxiety was less after intervention for the experimental group showing the effect of relaxation, meditation, and visualization.

(b) Comparison of Depression Scores of Experimental and Control Groups of CHD Patients After Intervention:

For the variable Depression, the mean value for the experimental group was 34.71 after intervention and for the control group after the intervention period were 36.89. The standard deviations were 4.27 and 4.63 respectively. The t-value obtained was -2.68. The details of the t-test are given in Table 17.

TABLE 17

After intervention scores of experimental and control groups:
Results of t-test for depression

Depression	Mean	SD	t-value	Level of Significance
Experimental Group	34.71	4.27	-2.68	0.01
Control Group	36.89	4.63		

Note: The t-value is significant statistically.

The results indicated that there was significant difference between the scores for the variable Depression, for the experimental and control groups after intervention. This means that the level of Depression was less after intervention for the experimental group, showing the effect of relaxation, meditation, and visualization.

(c) Comparison of Security Feeling Scores of Experimental and Control Groups of CHD Patients After Intervention:

For the variable Security Feeling, the mean value for the experimental group was 56.13after intervention and for the control group after the intervention period was 54.07. The standard deviations were 3.27 and 5.03 respectively. The t-value obtained was 2.66. The details of the t-test are given in Table 18.

TABLE 18

After intervention scores of experimental and control groups:
Results of t-test for security feeling

Security Feeling	Mean	SD	t-value	Level of Significance
Experimental Group	56.13	3.27	2.66	0.01
Control Group	54.07	5.03		

Note: The t-value is significant statistically.

The results indicated that there was significant difference between the scores for the variable Security Feeling, for the experimental and control groups after intervention. This means that the level of Security Feeling was increased after intervention for the experimental group, showing the effect of relaxation, meditation, and visualization.

(d) Comparison of Stress Tolerance Scores of Experimental and Control Groups of CHD Patients After Intervention:

For the variable Stress Tolerance, the mean value for the experimental group was 64.73 after intervention and for the control group after the intervention period was 56.13. The standard deviations were 13.18 and 3.27 respectively. The t-value obtained was 5.64. The details of the t-test are given in Table 19.

TABLE 19

After intervention scores of experimental and control groups:
Results of t-test for stress tolerance

Stress Tolerance	Mean	SD	t-value	Level of Significance
Experimental Group	64.73	3.27	5.64	0.01
Control Group	56.13	13.18		

Note: The t-value is significant statistically.

The results indicated that there was significant difference between the scores for the variable Stress Tolerance, for the experimental and control groups after intervention. This means that the level of Stress Tolerance was increased after intervention for the experimental group showing the effect of relaxation, meditation, and visualization.

(e) Comparison of Quality of Life Scores of and Groups of CHD Patients After Intervention:

For the variable Quality of Life, the mean value for the experimental group was 114.67 after intervention and for the control group after the intervention period was 108.51. The standard deviations were 16.49 and 15.81 respectively. The t-value obtained was 5.64.

The details of the t-test are given in Table 20.

TABLE 20

After intervention scores of experimental and control groups: Results of t-test for quality of life

Quality of Life	Mean	SD	t-value	Level of Significance
Experimental Group	114.67	16.49	5.64	0.01
Control Group	108.51	15.81		

Note: The t-value is significant statistically.

The results indicated that there was significant difference between the scores for the variable Quality of Life, for the experimental and control groups after intervention. This means that the level of Quality of Life increased after intervention for the experimental group showing the effect of relaxation, meditation, and visualization.

Summary of Results of the t-tests

The results given above indicate that the following three sets of analyses have been done using t-tests:

1. Comparison of pretest and post test data of experimental group.
2. Comparison of pretest data of experimental and control groups
3. Comparison of posttest data of experimental and control groups

Here, both the groups of subjects were coronary heart disease patients. The variables used for comparison were anxiety, depression, security feeling, stress tolerance, and quality of life. All these variables remained the same in both the groups initially.

For the first two variables, there was reduction in the scores after intervention, whereas for the latter three variables there was increase, as for as the experimental group is concerned.

C. CORRELATION ANALYSIS

The correlation coefficients among the variables used in the study are given in Table 21.

TABLE 21

Intercorrelations among the five variables of CHD patients before intervention (N=120)

Variable	Correlation Coefficients (r)				
	1	2	3	4	5
1. Anxiety	( )	+0.208 *	-0.319 **	-0.230 *	+0.284 **
2. Depression	..	( )	-0.382 **	-0.334 **	-0.212 *
3. Security Feeling	..	..	( )	+0.419 **	+0.520 **
4. Stress Tolerance	..	..	..	( )	+0.492 **
5. Quality of Life	..	..	..	..	( )

Note : ** indicates that r is significant at 0.01 level.

* indicates that r is significant at 0.05 level.

It may be seen from Table 21 that out of the ten r's reported among the five variables of the coronary heart disease patients, seven r's were siginificant at 0.01 level, and three r's were significant at 0.05 level. It may also be seen that five of these r's were positive and five were negative.

These r's are described below.

1. *Correlation between Anxiety and Depression :*

It was found that the correlation between anxiety and depression is + 0.208 (vide Table 21). This is very low, showing that there is positive but low relation between anxiety and depression of CHD patients. As anxiety increases, the depression also increases, slightly. The percentage overlap between anxiety and depression was 4.326 (r^2 x 100). This means that only 4.326 per cent is the shared variance.

2. *Correlation between Anxiety and Security Feeling :*

The r between anxiety and security feeling of CHD patients was – 0.319, as given in Table 21. This is very low, and negative, showing that when anxiety increases, there is a slight decrease in security feeling. The percentage overlap between anxiety and security feeling was 10.176. This means that 10.176 per cent is the shared variance between anxiety and security feeling.

3. Correlation between Anxiety and Stress Tolerance :

Table 21 indicates that the coefficient of correlation between anxiety and stress tolerance was - 0.230. This is very low, showing that there is negative but low relation between anxiety and stress tolerance. This correlation coefficient shows that as anxiety increases, stress tolerance decreases, though at a low level. Here, the percentage overlap was 5.29. This means that only 5.29 per cent is the shared variance between anxiety and stress tolerance of CHD patients.

4. Correlation between Anxiety and Quality of life :

The r obtained between anxiety and quality of life was + 0.284, as per Table 21. This is low, showing that there is positive but low relation between anxiety and quality of life. The percentage overlap obtained was 8.06. This means that only 8.06 per cent is the shared variance between anxiety and quality of life.

5. Correlation between Depression and Security Feeling :

The coefficient correlation obtained between depression and security feeling was – 0.382 (vide Table 21). This r was low and negative, and shows that as the depression increases there is a low decrease in the security feeling of CHD patients. Percentage overlap between depression and security feeling was 14.59, indicating that only 14.59 per cent is the shared variance.

5. Correlation between Depression and Stress Tolerance :

It is seen from Table 21 that the r between depression and stress tolerance was – 0.334. This is low and negative correlation. As the variable depression increases, the capacity to tolerate stress decreases, to a small extent. Here, the percentage overlap was 11.15. This means that only 11.15 per cent is the shared variance between depression and stress tolerance.

6. Correlation between Depression and Quality of life:

The correlation coefficient obtained between depression and quality of life for the CHD patient, as given in Table 21, was –0.212. This shows that there is negative, but low relation between depression and quality of life. Percentage overlap between depression and quality of life was 4.49. This means that only 4.49 per cent is the shared variance between the two variables.

7. Correlation between Security Feeling and Stress Tolerance :

Table 21 shows that the coefficient of correlation between security feeling and stress tolerance was + 0.419. This shows that there is positive and marked relation between the variables, for the CHD patients. As one variable increases the other also increases. Here, the percentage overlap was 17.55. This means that only 17.55 per cent is the shared variance between security feeling and stress tolerance.

8. Correlation between Security Feeling and Quality of Life :

It is found from Table 21 that the r between security feeling and quality of life was + 0.520. Here also the correlation is positive and marked, showing that when security feeling increases quality of life, also increases substantially. Here, the percentage overlap was 27.04, indicating that only 27.04 per cent is the shared variance between security feeling and quality of life for the CHD patients.

9. Correlation between Stress Tolerance and Quality of Life:

The correlation between stress tolerance and quality of life was + 0.492. This denotes a positive and marked relationship. As the variable, security feeling increases, the other variable, quality of life also increases to a substantial degree. Here, the percentage overlap was 24.2, indicating that 24.2 per cent is the shared variance between security feeling and quality of life.

The summary of the variables correlated, r , and interpretation are given in Table 22.

TABLE 22

Interpretation of r's among the five variables

Sl. No.	Variables correlated	r	Level of significance	Nature of r	Verbal Interpretation
1	Security feeling and Quality of Life	+0.520	0.01	Positive	Substantial or marked
2	Stress tolerance and Quality of Life	+0.492	0.01	Positive	Substantial or marked
3	Security feeling and Stress tolerance	+0.419	0.01	Positive	Substantial or marked
4	Depression and Security feeling	- 0.382	0.01	Negative	Low : present but slight
5	Depression and Stress tolerance	- 0.334	0.01	Negative	Low : present but slight
6	Anxiety and Security feeling	- 0.319	0.01	Negative	Low : present but slight
7	Anxiety and Quality of Life	+0.284	0.01	Positive	Low : present but slight
8	Anxiety and Stress tolerance	- 0.230	0.05	Negative	Low : present but slight
9	Depression and Quality of Life	- 0.212	0.05	Negative	Low : present but slight
10	Anxiety and Depression	+0.208	0.05	Positive	Low : present but slight

D. CASE STUDY: THE PRESENTATION AND COMMENTS

The present investigator had experience with coronary heart disease patients, as she was working as Family Counsellor on part time basis ever since she completed her Master's degree course in Psychology. She could contact patients in different areas of clinical psychology, especially those suffering from heart problems.

The patients came to know about the intervention programme from other heart patients who had undergone this treatment procedure and also from other sources. The concerned Cardiologist referred such patients with psychosomatic diseases to the family counsellor.

The experience of the present investigator is that patients with more severe stress have been shown to develop more severe coronary heart diseases. It is now well-realized that the effect of any stress depends upon its perception by the individual. In other words, what a person makes of that situation is important. Research has also revealed that mental stress, either acute or chronic, produces certain physiological responses via the central nervous system. These physiological responses consist of increase in heart rate, blood pressure, increased coronary constriction and increased platelet activity.

I have used clinical interview and observation for studying the patients. Due to my close interaction with the patients and their relatives, they provided important information like the behaviour, relationship, and how the patient faces the stress situation. It is obvious that without controlling the stresses, we cannot stop the progress of CHD. Sudden stress or anger leads to the spasm of coronary arteries which precipitates sudden angina and heart attacks. This is the reason or mechanism why many people develop heart attacks when they are excessively strained or hear a bad news.

Most of the young heart patients of modern times have Type A behaviour. These particular types of people who are aggressive, always having short of time, short tempered and stressful are more prone to develop heart disease. Negative emotions such as anger, hatred, resentment, jealousy, pride, egoism, anxiety, depression, and insecurity result in chronically elevated levels of stress hormones. The positive emotions like love, care, compassion, and altruism promote healing to good health and longevity.

Heart disease is treated in a number of ways. For many people, CHD can be managed with surgery or angioplasty, and others with medications. Here, in the hospital, we are using the lifestyle modification programme, which consists of progressive relaxation, meditation, and visualization. There are individual, group, and family counseling sessions as well. This programme promotes the health of the patient and his immune system, and makes the body strong enough to face any stressful situations, thereby correcting the impaired physical, emotional, and social functions. It may be remembered that, once heart develops this disease, it requires life long management.

The present investigator felt that case studies of coronary heart disease patients would be much use to the Cardiologist, in the sense that innumerable factors or variables may be associated with psychosomatic diseases. Hence, the present investigator felt that two case studies will be of use to highlight at least certain problems related to CHD patients, in addition to the data collected through psychological tests.

Two cases of coronary heart disease patients who had undergone intervention programme are presented below.

CASE 1

Mr. X was born to lower middle class parents in a remote Village of Trichur district in 1950. He joined a local school and completed his tenth standard at the age of 14. He had a flair for stage performance during his school days. He had also acted in school dramas several times.

After his school days he took up the job as a watch repairer to support his aged parents. In addition to the repair job, he pursued his favourite hobby of acting whenever he got a chance.

By the time he was about 24, he set up a small troupe under the banner "UDAYA" and provided technical services like sound, light and other services for make up and stage arrangements to local drama clubs. It was a great success and he could earn enough money to have his own family. Subsequently he married a middle class girl who had studied up to the eighth standard. She was very happy and could manage the family well. Their married life was very happy. They had two boys and two girls.

By the time he was 40, he suffered some breathing problems and some other ailments and he stopped the habit of chain smoking that had been his habit for the post 20-25 years. He had also muscle pain and was unable to bicycle for his errands. He had been to his friend and family doctor for a check up. During the examination, it was found that he was under high cholesterol and advised to follow strict dietary control.

Later on, he took up a job as a watch repairer in a Gulf country. He had been there for about 6 years. One evening he felt a sudden shooting pain on his left hand and was unable to raise his hand. He was immediately rushed to a hospital about 400 kms. away. After a thorough check up, the doctor informed him that his cholesterol level was very high. He had also undergone ECG, TMT etc. Being a Government hospital, he could avail free treatment for about 4-5 weeks. However, the treatment in the hospital in Gulf did not cure his illness completely. He still suffered from pain and congestion in the chest. He decided to return to India.

On his arrival in India, he revived his old troupe "Udaya", and provided various service to professional drama troupes.

On one morning, at the age of 55, he suffered angina, as he lifted a bucket of water in the bathroom. Same day evening he consulted his family doctor. The doctor advised him to see a cardiologist at the earliest. Mr. X got admitted on the same day in a well known hospital at Trichur. Duty doctor examined him without delay, and put him in Intensive Care Unit. Since that was a Sunday, the Cardiologist was not immediately available. The Cardiologist examined him on Monday morning and told him that this was his second attack, probably the first one was a silent attack, went unnoticed. After detailed check up like TMT, Scan etc., for a week, he was discharged from the Hospital and told to continue the medicines regularly. He was also advised to avoid food prepared in oil, meat preparations and milk products.

Although Mr. X was suffering from frequent pain in the chest, he was irregular for routine medical checkup ignoring the danger of another heart attack. The condition continues to worsen. However, he consulted the Cardiologist again when the pain became severe. The Doctor told him that his condition worsened further and the only solution is a by-pass surgery as early as possible. He prescribed some medicines for a month and told him to come prepared for by-pass.

Meanwhile, he handed over the management of his troupe to his eldest son as his health deteriorated. Although he was suffering from heart problems he had never experienced any sort of death anxiety. This was mainly because he had been working on live wire because the electricity could not be switched off almost all the time especially for programs in temples and churches before his work, fully realizing the danger of electric shock. Even when his generators were stolen, he kept his grounds. He was very moody. He was tight all the time. He even learned that his blood vessels were tight and restricted.

Then he came to the Life Style Modification Programme by Dr. Eraly at PNVM hospital, Ernakulam on persuasion by his family members. He participated in it. He strictly followed the relaxation, meditation and visualization techniques as per the advice of the doctor, along with the medicines. When one meditates, the brain wave pattern reduces its frequency to what is called alpha activity. It is noted that when an individual achieves the relaxation, slow rhythmic alpha activity is recorded from the frontal lobe of the brain. Various chemical changes occurring in the body promote healing by increasing the immune status of the individual. He is told to visualize their coronary arteries, where blockages occur. Then he visualizes the blockages dissolving, or disappearing.

After six weeks, he find himself inclining towards improvement. By doing all this, he controlled his weight/cholesterol etc. After that he have not experienced angina at any time, even he had not taken the sorbitrate tablets. He is feeling a lot of improvement physically and mentally. He feel very confident and comfortable. With this programme he was able to reduce his medicine and weight as well. He is feeling fit himself. Now with the guidance and advice he is getting used to routine stress management techniques. He is now leading a normal life. Now he can walk for about 2 km without strain or heaviness in the chest. He is able to resume his day to day activities. He never has chest pain.

He has got so much satisfaction that he encouraged others also to join the programme. After eight months, he has done the TMT again. To his surprise, the TMT showed negative results. That means, the heart disease is reversed. His medicines were reduced and he never got angina after the programme.

Comments:

Mr. X was very depressed and he lost the happiness in the life. This patient with high depression had shown to develop more severe CHD. He felt heaviness, tightness, frequent pain in the arms, neck, and jaws. He had the feeling of insecurity; his quality of life was low. The studies had shown that this type of negative feeling has an adverse effect on CHD patients. Furthermore, depression or anxiety may result in chronically elevated levels of stress hormones. The relatives of the patients also provided important information about the change in his mood and behaviour.

After attending the intervention programme, his chest pain vanished completely, serum cholesterol dropped, blood pressure stabilized, and medications were reduced or eliminated. He began to lose weight and report a renewed sense of confidence and control. His level of security feeling as well as quality of life got increased, whereas depression got reduced after intervention. Studies showed that the positive emotions of caring, love, and compassion promote healing to good health and longevity. In his case also, his wife and children were supportive, and helped him to come back to his routine life, facilitating his physical, mental, and spiritual wellness. And many of these changes became apparent within a short period of time.

His TreadMill Test result indicated the improvement in the disease. Whereas the TMT result showed strongly positive at two minutes before intervention, it became negative in 15 minutes time after intervention.

CASE 2

Mr. Y was born in a lower middle class family of Valloor Village in Mahe on 28th June 1949 to Puthenpurayil Sankaran and Mathu. He had one older brother and three sisters.

He could not recollect anything about his life style and other family history upto the age of 5. However he is definite that he had his schooling from first standard to metric in a high school situated in Valloor Village. On completion of his metric he joined a commercial institute and qualified in typewriting and shorthand by the age of 23. After that he completed Degree in science.

His elder brother who was working as a Government servant died in 1974 and Mr. Y got a small job in Government service under "died in harness scheme" in February 1975. Subsequently his father also died in 1978.

Mr. Y got married to a "pre-degree completed" girl on 29th June 1980. A baby girl was born in November, 1981 to them. They were overjoyed with the new arrival. When his daughter was 6 months old, his wife joined a Government college in Mahe and completed her graduation. His wife was very much interested in securing a job at the earliest so that their family can have a smooth sailing. With this in mind Mr. Y managed a transfer to Pondicherry. Subsequently they shifted their family to Pondicherry, capital of Mahe in June, 1986.

On settling down at Pondicherry his wife appeared for a clerical test in the same year and got selected as a Lower Division Clerk on temporary basis. By December 1987, she was made permanent. Meanwhile he also got a promotion.

In order to develop his daughter's talents, Mr. Y got her admitted to a dance class, when she was in her sixth standard.

He was very much attached to her daughter. He was over anxious on all her activities. He himself used to take her to school and also to dance classes. By that time she got interested in sports. She was encouraged by her parents by arranging special coaching in Table Tennis and Badminton. She had represented Pondicherry State in national level she participated in games at Jaipur, Assam and Hyderabad. They always made it a point to accompany their daughter so that she will always be with them. On her completion of plus two course, she got admission in a Government Engineering College at Salem, a place which is about 6 hours journey from Pondicherry.

In the mean time, Mr. Y became a diabetic patient from 1995. He had consulted various doctors and was under their treatment.

On her joining in the Engineering College, the daughter had to leave her parents and stay in the college hostel away from home. As Mr. Y was very much attached to his daughter, her absence from house had saddened him and caused mental tension. He was very anxious about his daughter. And this anxiety made him sick. She also suffered from home sickness, and could not concentrate in studies. To overcome this problem and facilitate frequent meeting with their daughter, he hired a house near her college. On weekends and public holidays they used to stay with their daughter in that rented house. After one year, they vacated the rented house, and used to travel on week - ends from Pondicherry to meet her and return on the same day.

During this time, Mr. Y's wife got a promotion and their financial status had improved very much. They could build a new spacious house at their native village during this period. They found it as a good asset.

Then on one morning about 4 o' clock on 6th September 2001 he experienced a chest pain. Immediately he was admitted to a Government hospital at Pondicherry. On discharge from that hospital, he consulted a Cardiologist at JIPMER hospital in Pondicherry. They conducted various tests including Tread Mill Test (TMT). In TMT result, they remarked positive, (which means that there is block in coronary arteries). Medication continued regularly. Later on, he used to feel some sort of weight on his chest. Again, he contacted the cardiologist at

JIPMER hospital, who advised that blocks if any, can be confirmed by an Angiogram. (Though the Angiogram test is not essential, it is usually followed in specialized hospitals.)

On his advice he went to Appolo hospital, Chennai and underwent Angiogram. The results were shown to the cardiologist at JIPMER and he confirmed that there are blocks in his arteries i.e. one is 90 percent and other is 45 percent. However he told Mr. Y that the present situation does not need a bypass surgery, but an Angioplasty might be done. He was worried as to how he will over come from this great problem. The doctor had also referred this case to Amrutha hospital, Ernakulam for a detailed study.

Soon Mr. Y went to Amrutha hospital and consulted the cardiologist. The Cardiologist at Amrutha hospital agreed with the opinion of the cardiologist at JIPMER. The doctor had suggested getting Angioplasty first, if blockages reoccur then to have Bypass Surgery to remove blockages. He was suffering from breathlessness and palpitation, and was unable to sit, walk, and eat and led a tiring life.

On hearing this, he discussed the matter with his wife and decided to consult Dr. George Eraly, a famous Cardiologist who practices the reversal of heart diseases by the Life Style Modification Programme at PNVM hospital, at Ernakulam. There is no need for surgery or Angioplasty, if one practices the programme for reversal of heart diseases.

Then they consulted Dr. G. Eraly at PNVM hospital. He has carried out detailed tests. However the doctor advised him to contact some of his patients who had already undergone the treatment, and if really interested, contact him again at PNVM hospital without much delay. Thus, as per Dr. Eraly's instructions, Mr. Y got admitted at PNVM hospital on 28th December 2001. The doctor assured him that there is no need of any angioplasty/surgery.

He joined the programme . He stayed there for about 12 days. Before joining the programme he could barely walk 100 yards without feeling breathless. He was very much depressed and worried. He is already an anxious person. His anxiety increased when his daughter had gone to join the Engineering degree. He was under a lot of emotional stress at that time. After attending this programme, he has been doing regular stress management techniques like relaxation, meditation and visualization. After the programme, he felt a release of tension. He felt good. In his version he says, "I just felt a release. I felt, this is what life is all about. It's made me feel better. Now I think I'll face some other things in this group. This group is helping me. And when I opened up, they opened up. Instead of rejecting me, we all felt a lot closer".

He has reduced his weight 24 kgs, previously his weight was 92 kgs and now it is 68 kgs which is normal for his height. Now he can attend to his normal activities without any problem. He can assure that this programme has improved his health. He feels better and the occasional tightness in his chest has disappeared. The Cardiologist has reduced medications. He now have a sense of well-being, after starting the programme and his quality of life has also improved both at home and in the office.

He is very much thankful to doctor and the staff of PNVM Hospital, Ernakulam. After one year, he again underwent the tests, and he is fully satisfied with the results. His Treadmill Test became negative in addition to discontinuing insulin totally.

Comments:

Stress is such an influential risk factor that even in the absence of other risk factors it can itself become responsible for coronary hearty disease. Mr. Y. was overstressed with a lack of social support. he felt isolated because his daughter was studying in another place. Stress is such an important factor that his excessive stress lead to increase in his blood pressure and increase in the heart rate. There are many people like him, without high cholesterol, or without family history developing angina only because of excessive stress.

He was willing to undergo the Ornish's Lifestyle modification programme, he got benefit from it. He got trained in Ornish's techniques of stress management, including breathing techniques, meditation, visualization and progressive relaxation. By this, his level of stress tolerance got increased, and had a better security feeling and good quality of life. This would help them to interact with others in a more meaningful way.

This shows the effectiveness of the intervention programme on Mr.Y. Due to this, he and his family members are very much benefitted.

By attending this intervention programmes regularly, the patients will be able to reduce their anxiety and depression and increase the stress tolerance, security feeling, and quality of life. The results of the TreadMill Test indicated that, in the case of Mr. Y., there was a great difference between the TMT taken before the intervention (result was positive at 3 minutes), and after the intervention (result was positive at 12 minutes).

E. TREADMILL TEST (STRESS ELECTROCARDIOGRAPHY)

Patients with coronary artery blockages may have minimal symptoms and an unremarkable or unchanged ECG while at rest. Alternatively, patients with no heart disease may have fairly convincing symptoms and a suspicious ECG. Both groups may benefit from a cardiac stress test during which exercise is used to stress the heart and expose hidden heart disease or to help rule it out.

The heart may be stressed by having a patient exercise on a treadmill or a stationary bicycle. If the patient is unable to exercise secondary to physical limitations such as severe arthritis, artificial limbs, generalized weakness, paralysis, unsteady gait, etc., the physician may choose a pharmacological or chemical form of test.

Stress testing, particularly those employing exercise, help reveal the following :

The length of exercise demonstrates physical tolerance and conditioning. Extreme and inappropriate shortness of breath, chest discomfort, dizziness and unexpected weakness may suggest underlying heart disease. The blood pressure is recorded at intervals during stress (in the beginning and usually at three minute intervals, if stable). It may be checked more frequently if the patient's blood pressure response to exercise is abnormal. High blood pressure during exercise may provide an early clue or indication about this problem. Normally, the systolic (upper reading) blood pressure may rise up to 200 during extreme or peak exercise, while the diastolic (lower reading) remains below 90. Patients with inadequately controlled high blood pressure usually display high diastolic readings during exercise. A drop in blood pressure during exercise may indicate heart disease. Exercise may provoke arrhythmias or irregular heart rhythm which may not be seen at rest and may or may not point to heart disease. The ECG is constantly monitored during exercise and recorded on paper at intervals (usually every minute) and compared to the ECG obtained at rest.

The risk of cardiac stress testing is very small. Since it is carried out in patients with known or suspected heart disease, almost every lab is also equipped with emergency cardiac drugs and resuscitative equipment. It is emphasized that these are precautionary measures that are rarely needed.

During stress testing, the heart rhythm is constantly displayed on a heart monitor. This allows the physician to keep an eye on the patient's heart rate, and to watch out for telltale ECG changes and irregular heart rhythm. When a treadmill or stationary bicycle stress testing is conducted, it is continued until the patient achieves a target heart rate (based upon age). However, it may be stopped early if the patient develops significant symptoms (chest pain, extreme shortness of breath, weakness, leg fatigue, dizziness, etc.), serious irregular heart rhythm or marked elevation of blood pressure. It is emphasized the majority of patient's do not develop these problems. Fatigue, as would be expected after a good workout, is the only residual complaint.

The treadmill is started at a relatively slow "warm-up" speed. The treadmill speed and it's slope or inclination are increased every three minutes according to a preprogrammed protocol. The protocol dictates the precise speed and slope. Each three minute interval is known as a Stage (Stage 1, Stage 2, Stage 3, etc. Thus a patient completing Stage 3 has exercised for 3 x 3 = 9 minutes). The patient's blood pressure is usually recorded during the second minute of each stage.

The ECG is constantly displayed on the monitor. It is also recorded on paper at one minute intervals. The physician pays particular attention to the heart rate, blood pressure, changes in the ECG pattern, irregular heart rhythm, and the patient's appearance and symptoms. The treadmill is stopped when the patient achieves a target heart rate (this is 85 % of the maximal heart rate predicted for the patient's age). However, if the patient is doing extremely well at peak exercise, the treadmill test may be continued further. The test may be stopped prior to achievement of the target heart rate if the patient develops significant chest discomfort, shortness of breath, dizziness, unsteady gait, etc., or if the ECG shows alarming changes or serious irregular heart beats.

(***Heart site.com.*** - Source: Internet).

A diagrammatic representation of Treadmill results of CHD patients is given in Figure 3.

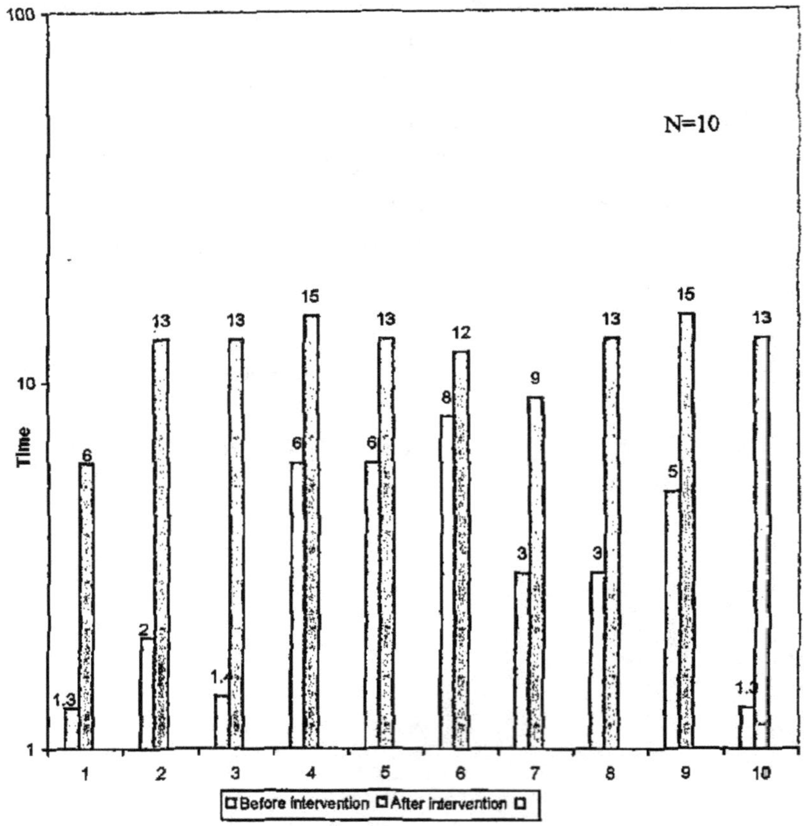

Fig. 3. Diagrammatic representation of treadmill results of CHD patients

CHAPTER V

SUMMARY AND CONCLUSIONS

A. Resume of the investigation
B. Test of tenability of the hypotheses
C. Important findings
D. Implications
E. Limitations of the present study
F. Suggestions for further research

A. RESUME OF THE INVESTIGATION

Coronary Heart Disease (CHD), also known as Coronary Artery Disease or Ischaemic Heart Disease, is now proving to be one of the leading causes of morbidity and mortality throughout the world. While in the west, the number of persons developing CHD is decreasing, the opposite still holds true in India.

The main cause of this disease is deposition of cholesterol and fat in the inner smooth lining of the blood vessels (coronary arteries) supplying blood to the heart resulting in their blockages and obstruction to blood flow through them. With significant blockages, and exertion, the increased demand of blood by the heart is not met. A sensation of pain is felt and the heaviness or pain in the left side of the chest, (called angina) typically radiates to the left arm. It may be associated with sweating, choking sensation, and breathlessness. Psychological Stress or Tension is now recognized as the most important risk factor of coronary heart disease. There are many people without high cholesterol, over weight, and family history, having normal blood pressure developing angina only because of excessive stress.

Bypass surgery and angioplasty are the most accepted techniques for curing heart diseases. Now, a growing body of research has shown that heart disease can be cured without surgery. The first evidence that lifestyle changes alone – no drugs, no surgery- can set heart disease patients on the road to improved health appeared in a study directed by Dr. Dean Ornish (1996). Based on his internationally acclaimed scientific study, which has now been ongoing for a few years, Dr. Ornish's programme has yielded amazing results. Stress management sessions are major component of Ornish's programme. Each session is led by an instructor trained in Ornish's techniques of stress management, including stretching exercises, breathing techniques, meditation, creative visualization, and progressive relaxation. Effectively managing emotional stress not only helps eliminate one of the risk factors involved in heart disease, but helps encourage physical, mental, and spiritual wellness.

The present investigation is intended to study the effect of the above programme on coronary heart disease patients. The study emphasizes relaxation, meditation, and visualization.

Sample:

A sample of sixty coronary heart disease patients were selected from PNVM Hospital at Ernakulam, on the basis of the tests conducted by Cardiologist, for confirming coronary heart disease. These subjects were given intervention programme. A control group of sixty coronary heart disease patients who were not given intervention programme were also selected for comparative purposes. The age range of both the groups varied between 30-55 years. Both the groups were given routine medicines, by the cardiologist.

Variables:

The variables used for the investigation to study the effect of intervention programmes on coronary heart disease patients were anxiety, depression, security feeling, stress tolerance, and quality of life.

Data Collection Procedure:

(1) *Psychological tests and intervention programme* : With the help of standardized psychological tests, data on relevant variables were collected from the subjects, before intervention in the case of both the groups (Pre-test data). The subjects in the experimental group (intervention group) were given systematic training programmes on relaxation, meditation, and visualization for 10-15 days. These subjects were informed of the importance of the programme and were asked to continue the same as a life long procedure to be followed daily without fail. The posttest data were collected after eight months of the commencement of the programme. The control group, viz., the non-intervention group (CHD patients without intervention but they are taking medicines only) were not given the training in intervention. However, the data from the control group were also taken before and after, while the data were taken from the experimental group.

(2) *Case Study* : On selected cases, interview was conducted for obtaining adequate information from the subjects as part of case study. The behaviour of the subjects was keenly observed by the investigator in order to establish adequate rapport, and to check the validity and reliability of their responses.

Analysis:

a. Quantitative :

The data were analysed and interpreted using :

(1). The t–test

(2). The Pearson r

b. Qualitative :

A few case studies were presented to obtain briefly sufficient information related to the heart problems and the effect of intervention programmes.

B. TEST OF TENABILITY OF THE HYPOTHESES

The major hypotheses formulated for the study were tested on the basis of the data and results discussed in the previous chapter, and the details are as follows:

(1) The first hypothesis that "There will be significant changes in anxiety, depression, security feeling, stress tolerance, and quality of life among coronary heart disease patients due to the intervention programme (relaxation, meditation, and visualization)" is accepted.

(2) The second hypothesis that "The inter correlations among anxiety, depression, security feeling, stress tolerance, and quality of life will be significant" is accepted.

C. IMPORTANT FINDINGS

(1). The result of the investigation indicated that there existed significant differences between experimental and control groups in all the variables under study.

(2). The correlations among the different variables under study were found to be significant statistically.

The details of the findings are given below under the variables used in the study :

a. Anxiety

The results indicated that there was significant difference between the scores for the variable Anxiety, for the CHD patients before and after intervention. This means that the level of anxiety got reduced after intervention, showing the effect of relaxation, meditation, and visualization on CHD patients.

There was no significant difference between the mean scores for the variable Anxiety obtained by the CHD patients and the control group before intervention. This indicates that the levels of Anxiety of both the experimental as well as the control group were the same, initially.

b. Depression

The results indicated that there was significant difference between the scores for the variable Depression, for the CHD patients before and after intervention. This means that the level of Depression got reduced after intervention, showing the effect of relaxation, meditation, and visualization on CHD patients. There was no significant difference between the mean scores for the variable Depression obtained by the CHD patients and the control group before intervention. This indicates that the levels of Depression of both the experimental as well as the control group were the same, initially.

c. Security Feeling

The results indicated that there was significant difference between the scores for the variable Security Feeling, for the CHD patients before and after intervention. This means that the level of Security Feeling got increased after intervention, showing the effect of relaxation, meditation, and visualization on CHD patients. There was no significant difference between the mean scores for the variable Security Feeling obtained by the CHD patients and the control group before intervention. This indicates that the levels of Security Feeling of both the experimental as well as the control group were the same, initially.

d. Stress Tolerance

The results indicated that there was significant difference between the scores for the variable Stress Tolerance, for the CHD patients before and after intervention. This means that the level of Stress Tolerance got increased after intervention, showing the effect of relaxation, meditation, and visualization on CHD patients.

The results indicated that there was no significant difference between the mean scores for the variable Stress Tolerance obtained by the CHD patients and the control group before intervention. This indicates that the levels of Security Feeling of both the experimental as well as the control group were the same, initially.

e. Quality of Life

The results indicated that there was significant difference between the scores for the variable Quality of Life, for the CHD patients before and after intervention. This means that the level of Quality of Life got increased after intervention, showing the effect of relaxation, meditation, and visualization on CHD patients.

There was no significant difference between the mean scores for the variable Quality of Life obtained by the CHD patients and the control group before intervention. This indicates that the levels of Quality of Life of both the experimental as well as the control group were the same, initially.

D. IMPLICATIONS OF THE STUDY

The implications of the investigation are many and varied. When the relevance of the present study in this context is considered, it can be said that all the findings of the present investigation can be of much help for those working with coronary heart disease patients, the family members who live with the patients, and others directly or indirectly related to the welfare of CHD patients.

a. *Implications for CHD Patients :*

Whoever may be the persons using the findings of this study, the final beneficiaries will be the CHD patients themselves. If they are aware of the intervention strategies, and are willing to undergo the same, they will benefit from it. This will help them to interact with others in a more meaningful way. Their anxiety and depression may get reduced. Their level of stress tolerance will be increased, and will lead to have better security feeling and good quality of life.

b. *Implications for family members of CHD Patients :*

The present study has shown the effectiveness of the intervention programme on CHD patients, and due to this their family members are very much benefited. By attending this intervention programmes regularly CHD patients will be able to reduce their anxiety and depression and increase the stress tolerance, security feeling, and quality of life. This will reflect on the family members.

c. *Implication for Cardiologists, Psychologists, Counsellors, and Social Workers :*

Besides what has been said above, this programme can be of immense value for Cardiologists, Psychologists, Counsellors and Social Workers. They can initiate steps so that the CHD patients will undergo the programme with the support of all who are concerned about the future of the patients.

d. *Implication towards Awareness Prgramme :*

In order to be more beneficial to common people, a general awareness has to be created by means of mass communication. For this purpose, services of print/electronic media will play a significant role. In addition to this, regular medical camps/ awareness programmes can be organized with the help of various clubs such as Lions/Rotary etc. Regular visits by social workers/counselors to old age homes, church parishes and other social functions will be useful for educating the people about CHD and intervention methods.

As per WHO reports, stated earlier, the approximate number of CHD patients expected to be a whopping figure of 70 lakhs by 2020. To meet this exigency Cardiologists, Counsellors, and major hospitals will have to put in more efforts to organise regular intervention programmes in a phased manner. It is suggested that major heart hospitals should make earnest endeavor to set up special departments consisting Cardiologists, Counsellors and Social Workers solely for this programme.

By having intensive intervention programmes, CHD patients can avoid costly treatment, tests, surgeries and thereby alleviating their financial burdens. Once this is achieved, the relatives of CHD patients will be at ease and stress experienced by them can be reduced to minimum.

During the awareness programme several information-providing strategies can be employed. "A test of a healthy heart" may be one of them. The details are shown below.

A TEST OF A HEALTHY HEART

How does your heart measure up? Check it out with this simple test. The numbers 1, 2, 3 etc in the boxes, represent your score and should be added up as you move from age to sex down to history. For example, if you are 35 years of age start with 3 points; if you are male, add 5; and 15 Ibs overweight, add 2. Go on down the chart till you get your final score, which is interpreted below.

(Devised by the Michigan Heart Association USA)

AGE	10 to 20 1	21 to 30 2	31 to 40 3	41 to 50 4	51 to 60 5	61 to 70 and over 8
SEX	Female under 40 1	Female 40-50 2	Female Over 50 3	Male 5	Stocky male 6	Bald stocky male 7
WEIGHT	More than 5lb below standard weight 0	-5 to +5lb standard weight 1	6-20lb overweight 2	21-35lb Overweight 3	36-50lb overweight 5	51-65lb overweight 7
FAT IN DIET	Diet contains no animal or solid fats 1	Diet contains 10% animal or solid fats 2	Diet contains 20% animal or solid fats 3	Diet contains 30% animal or solid fats 4	Diet contains 40% animal or solid fats 5	Diet contains 50% animal or solid fats 7
EXERCISE	Intensive work and recreational exertion 2	Moderate work and recreational exertion 2	Sedentary work and intense recreational exertion 3	Sedentary work and moderate recreational exertion 5	Sedentary work and light recreational exertion 6	Complete lack of all exercise 8
SMOKING	Non-user 0	Cigar and/or pipe 1	10 Cigarettes or less a day 2	20 Cigarettes a day 4	30 Cigarettes a day 6	40 Cigarettes a day or more 10
BLOOD PRESSURE	100 (upper reading) 1	120 (upper reading) 2	140 (upper reading) 3	160 (upper reading) 4	180 (upper reading) 6	200 or over (upper reading) 8
HISTORY	No known history of heart disease 1	1 relative over 60 with heart disease 2	2 relatives over 60 with heart disease 3	1 relative under 60 with heart disease 4	2 relatives under 60 with heart disease 6	3 relatives under 60 with heart disease 7

What your score means: 6-11 is well below the average risk; 12-17 is below average risk; 18-24 is the average risk; 25-31 represents a moderate risk; 32-40 represents a dangerous risk. If your total score is above this high-risk category, there is not necessarily any cause for concern but it would be worthwhile to consider seeing your doctor for advice.

(Reproduced from The illustrated London News, Feb. 1985)

E. LIMITATIONS OF THE PRESENT INVESTIGATION

1. The present study was conducted using a sample selected from only one district in the state of Kerala, namely Ernakulam.

2. The differences due to religion, caste, community and other socio-cultural conditions existing in other parts of the state may have an impact on the attitudes and perceptions of the individual. The results obtained in one state need not necessarily hold good for other states too. In this context, the generalization of the results of the present study may be made with caution.

3. The number of variables included in the present study was limited to five important ones. However, a wide variety of other equally important variables remain to be explored.

4. Statistical techniques such as regression analysis and factor analysis would have yielded a variety of results, which could strengthen the present findings.

F. SUGGESTIONS FOR FURTHER RESEARCH

The findings of the present study revealed the importance and utility of intervention strategies among coronary heart disease patients. The following are some of the suggestions for future research in the area.

1. The study may be replicated using a wider sample selected from all over the state, so that possible differences, if any, due to socio cultural variations can be understood. This will help to make comparisons as well as generalizations.

2. Studies may be conducted using anyone of the three programmes, viz., relaxation, meditation, and visualization on three comparable samples, and the effect of each can be compared.

3. In further studies in the area, three samples of CHD patients can be selected and two of the three intervention programmes can be applied on each. The first sample may undergo relaxation and meditation, the second sample relaxation and visualization, and the third meditation and visualization. The effect can be compared.

4. More intervention strategies such as the practice of Yoga, cognitive behavioural treatment, spiritual healing, music therapy, transcendental Meditation, in addition to relaxation, meditation, and visualization can be applied on further studies to understand the effect of new techniques on anxiety, depression, stress tolerance etc. of CHD patients.

5. Variables such as mental health status, inferiority, and feeling of well-being, emotional adjustment, and alienation can also be used in future studies, and the effect of intervention on these variables can be studied on CHD patients.

6. The effect of follow-up on patients who underwent relaxation, meditation, and visualization can be subjected to study in further investigation.

7. The research design in further studies can be formulated to use statistical techniques such as multivariate analysis of variance, and factor analysis. This will help to study the effect of intervention programme on a larger number of variables at a time.

The investigator would be gratified, if the results of the present investigation are used for further research and are made use of, by those involved in the welfare of Coronary heart disease patients and their families, like counselors, social workers and governmental agencies.

CPSIA information can be obtained
at www.ICGtesting.com
Printed in the USA
LVHW012114291122
734192LV00014B/583

9 781805 451877